W9-CKP-726

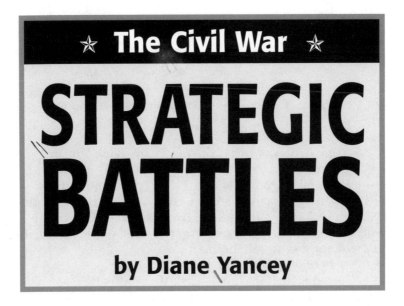

★ The Civil War ★

STRATEGIC BATTLES

by Diane Yancey

Lucent Books, P.O. Box 289011, San Diego, CA 92198-9011

Titles in The American War Library series include:

World War II
Hitler and the Nazis
Kamikazes
Leaders and Generals
Life as a POW
Life of an American Soldier in
  Europe
Strategic Battles in Europe
Strategic Battles in the Pacific
The War at Home
Weapons of War

The Civil War
Leaders of the North and South
Life Among the Soldiers and
  Cavalry
Lincoln and the Abolition of
  Slavery
Strategic Battles
Weapons of War

Library of Congress Cataloging-in-Publication Data

Yancey, Diane.
    Strategic battles of the Civil War / by Diane Yancey
        p.   cm.—(American war library series)
    Includes bibliographical references (p.   ) and index.
    1. Summary: Discusses some of the strategic battles of the
Civil War, including the battle at Antietam, the clash of the
Ironclads, the Battle of Gettysburg, the siege of Vicksburg, and
the well-known General Sherman's march.
    ISBN 1-56006-496-X (lib. bdg. alk. paper)
    1. United States—History—Civil War, 1861–1865—
Campaigns—Juvenile literature. [1. United States—History—
Civil War, 1861–1865—Campaigns.] I. Title. II. Series
E470.Y36   2000
973.7'3—dc21   98-26446
                                                        CIP

Copyright 2000 by Lucent Books, Inc.
P.O. Box 289011, San Diego, California 92198-9011

Printed in the U.S.A.

★ Contents ★

A Nation Forged by War

The United States, like many nations, was forged and defined by war. Despite Benjamin Franklin's opinion that "There never was a good war or a bad peace," the United States owes its very existence to the War of Independence, one to which Franklin wholeheartedly subscribed. The country forged by war in 1776 was tempered and made stronger by the Civil War in the 1860s.

The Texas Revolution, the Mexican-American War, and the Spanish-American War expanded the country's borders and gave it overseas possessions. These wars made the United States a world power, but this status came with a price, as the nation became a key but reluctant player in both World War I and World War II.

Each successive war further defined the country's role on the world stage. Following World War II, U.S. foreign policy redefined itself to focus on the role of defender, not only of the freedom of its own citizens, but also of the freedom of people everywhere. During the cold war that followed World War II until the collapse of the Soviet Union, defending the world meant fighting communism. This goal, manifested in the Korean and Vietnam conflicts, proved elusive, and soured the American public on its achievability. As the United States emerged as the world's sole superpower, American foreign policy has been guided less by national interest and more on protecting international human rights. But as involvement in Somalia and Kosovo prove, this goal has been equally elusive.

As a result, the country's view of itself changed. Bolstered by victories in World Wars I and II, Americans first relished the role of protector. But, as war followed war in a seemingly endless procession, Americans began to doubt their leaders, their motives, and themselves. The Vietnam War especially caused people to question the validity of sending its young people to die in places where they were not particularly wanted and for people who did not seem especially grateful.

While the most obvious changes brought about by America's wars have been geopolitical in nature, many other aspects of society have been touched. War often does not bring about change directly, but acts instead like the catalyst in a chemical reaction, accelerating changes already in progress.

Some of these changes have been societal. The role of women in the United States had been slowly changing, but World War II put thousands into the workforce and into uniform. They might have gone back to being housewives after the war, but equality, once experienced, would not be forgotten.

Likewise, wars have accelerated technological change. The necessity for faster airplanes and a more destructive bomb led to the development of jet planes and nuclear energy. Artificial fibers developed for parachutes in the 1940s were used in the clothing of the 1950s.

Lucent Books' American War Library covers key wars in the development of the nation. Each war is covered in several volumes, to allow for more detail, context, and to provide volumes on often neglected subjects, such as the kamikazes of World War II, or weapons used in the Civil War. As with all Lucent Books, notes, annotated bibliographies, and appendixes such as glossaries give students a launching point for further research. In addition, sidebars and archival photographs enhance the text. Together, each volume in The American War Library will aid students in understanding how America's wars have shaped and changed its politics, economics, and society.

Fort Sumter and Beyond

With a crash of cannon and a cheer from fiery Southerners, the Civil War began on April 12, 1861, when Confederate troops led by General Pierre G. T. Beauregard opened fire on Fort Sumter in Charleston Harbor. The fort was held by Major Robert Anderson (once Beauregard's artillery instructor at the U.S. Military Academy at West Point) and a small force of U.S. soldiers who refused to surrender federal property to an upstart band of rebels who dared challenge the authority of the United States of America.

The battle of Fort Sumter proved to be relatively insignificant in terms of holdings or fatalities, but when the first shells thudded into the battlements, America became involved in a conflict that changed everyone and everything. As historian William C. Davis writes, "The guns had spoken. . . . The Confederate cannon had sliced through the tangle of issues that reasonable men had failed to unsnarl for a half century and more. . . . To the immense relief of many, the men of the North and the South were finally free to settle their complex differences in the simplest way—by force of arms."[1]

Confederate troops bombard Fort Sumter in Charleston Harbor on April 12, 1861.

Roots of the Conflict

The beginning of the most terrible war in American history had been a long time in coming. The roots of the conflict could be traced back to the late 1700s, when the nation had begun to be divided by sectionalism and slavery. At that time, early settlers discovered that the fertile soil and

A New Era

Heroic and horrifying, the Civil War was one of the ultimate defining and shaping events in U.S. history, affecting the way people viewed their country, their government, and even themselves. Producers Ken and Ric Burns comment on the war's impact on America in Geoffrey Ward's *The Civil War, An Illustrated History*.

The Civil War has been given many names: the War Between the States, the War Against Northern Aggression, the Second American Revolution, the Lost Cause, the War of the Rebellion, the Brothers' War, the Late Unpleasantness. Walt Whitman called it the War of Attempted Secession. Confederate General Joseph Johnston called it the War *Against* the States. By whatever name, it was unquestionably the most important event in the life of the nation. It saw the end of slavery and the downfall of a southern planter aristocracy. It was the watershed of a new political and economic order, and the beginning of big industry, big business, big government. It was the first modern war and, for Americans, the costliest, yielding the most American casualties and the greatest domestic suffering, spiritually and physically. It was the most horrible, necessary, intimate, acrimonious, mean-spirited, and heroic conflict the nation has known.

mild climate of the South was ideal for growing crops such as tobacco and cotton. They brought in slaves to work their land and developed a slow-paced, agrarian society that placed emphasis on tradition, cultural pursuits, and gracious living. In the North, where land was rocky and temperatures cooler, people began to rely on industry and trade. They valued hard work and independence, and gradually became convinced that slavery was an unjust institution that robbed human beings of their freedom and was an offense against God's moral laws.

By the mid 1800s, the abolitionist cause—a movement to totally abolish slavery in the United States—had gained considerable strength in the North. Radicals such as John Brown, who led an ill-fated raid on Harpers Ferry in an attempt to start a slave rebellion in Virginia in 1859, stirred widespread support among ordinary Northern citizens. Southerners, on the other hand, became more convinced that their way of life would collapse, and their rights would be violated, if the government emancipated millions of blacks who worked the fields and embodied hundreds of millions of dollars in personal property.

Slavery was one of the most significant issues of the war, although the initial objective of the North was preservation of the Union. Lincoln had said on his first Inauguration Day, "I have no purpose, directly or indirectly, to interfere with the institution of slavery in the states where it

John Brown's support of the abolitionist cause took a violent turn when he led a raid on Harpers Ferry.

exists. I believe I have no lawful right to do so, and I have no inclination to do so."[2] In a short time, however, debate over the fate of 4 million blacks in the South grew in importance until it all but eclipsed the primary aim. On September 22, 1862, Lincoln issued the Emancipation Proclamation, freeing slaves in all states that had seceded. There was no going back. One general wrote that

> it was no longer a question of the Union as it was that was to be re-established. It was the Union as it should be—that is to say, washed clean from its original sin. . . . We

were no longer merely the soldiers of a political controversy. . . . [We] were now the missionaries of a great work of redemption, the armed liberators of millions. . . . The war was ennobled; the object was higher.[3]

The Greatest Evil

Lincoln's election in 1860 brought national division and controversy to a head, since Southerners were convinced that his desire to contain slavery was a first step toward abolishing it. The Richmond *Whig* wrote that his election was "undoubtedly the greatest evil that has ever befallen this country. But the mischief is done, and the only relief for the American people is to shorten sail . . . send down the top masts, and prepare for a hurricane."[4]

A storm was certainly brewing. South Carolina became the first state to secede from the Union in December 1860. In the next few months, Mississippi, Florida, Alabama, Georgia, Louisiana, Texas, Virginia, Tennessee, Arkansas, and North Carolina also chose to withdraw. Jefferson Davis was sworn in as the first president of the Confederate States of America in February, and Richmond, Virginia, was designated the Confederate capital three months later. Confederate political aims focused on the preservation of slavery and the emphasis of states' rights.

Lincoln had believed at first that secession was supported by only a handful of wealthy planters and would not be

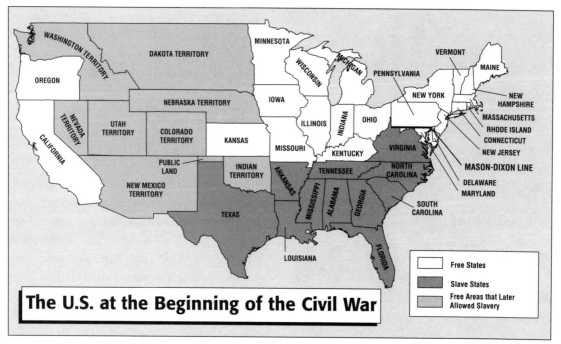

WASHINGTON TERRITORY

OREGON

DAKOTA TERRITORY

MINNESOTA

WISCONSIN

MICHIGAN

VERMONT

MAINE

PENNSYLVANIA

NEW YORK

NEW HAMPSHIRE

NEBRASKA TERRITORY

IOWA

NEVADA TERRITORY

UTAH TERRITORY

COLORADO TERRITORY

KANSAS

ILLINOIS

INDIANA

OHIO

MASSACHUSETTS

RHODE ISLAND

CONNECTICUT

NEW JERSEY

CALIFORNIA

MISSOURI

KENTUCKY

VIRGINIA

MASON-DIXON LINE

PUBLIC LAND

INDIAN TERRITORY

ARKANSAS

TENNESSEE

NORTH CAROLINA

DELAWARE

MARYLAND

NEW MEXICO TERRITORY

TEXAS

MISSISSIPPI

ALABAMA

GEORGIA

SOUTH CAROLINA

LOUISIANA

FLORIDA

The U.S. at the Beginning of the Civil War

Free States

Slave States

Free Areas that Later Allowed Slavery

defended by ordinary citizens. He was finally forced to accept that he would have to go to war to preserve the Union. Taking such a momentous step, however, required strong public support. That support soon came in response to the Southern attack on Sumter, one of four forts deep in Confederate territory that were still in federal hands.

"Strike a Blow!"

Robert Anderson, a Kentuckian who once owned slaves but believed strongly in "Duty, Honor, and Country," was in command at Fort Sumter, South Carolina, in 1861. Originally stationed at Fort Moultrie, just north of Sumter, Anderson had recognized the danger of being in enemy territory if war was declared, and

so he moved his men to the stronger fortress six days after South Carolina seceded from the Union. South Carolinians protested the move and demanded he return to Fort Moultrie. He refused, and the Southerners promptly cut off his supplies. From then on, Charleston Harbor had been ringed by Confederate guns, and the Federals sat as virtual prisoners, although no one had yet fired a shot.

In March, just two days after Lincoln's inauguration, Anderson sent word to Washington that his food supply was dwindling fast. If he was to hold the fort, he explained, the North would have to send him additional supplies, and that action could precipitate an armed strike from the South. Unsure of the wisest course of action, Lincoln finally signed an order on April 6, directing a relief expedition to sail south.

Hearing that a ship was on the way, Beauregard renewed his demands, shortly after midnight on April 12, that Anderson surrender. Anderson stalled, promising he would evacuate by noon of April 15 unless he received other instructions or supplies from the North. Since the Confederates had already sighted the supply ship off the coast, they decided that the time to strike was at hand.

At 4:00 A.M., the order was given to open fire. Congressman Roger Pryor, a Virginian who had publicly urged the South to "Strike a blow!"[5] two days before, was offered the chance to fire the first symbolic shot of the war, but at the last minute he realized the enormity of the action he was about to perform and refused. There was a short delay to find the proper representative. White-haired, sixty-seven-year-old Edmund Ruffin, a secessionist for twenty years, was awarded the honor. "Of course, I was highly gratified by the compliment, & delighted to perform the service,"[6] he said. At 4:30 A.M. the shell he fired streaked across the sky and slammed into the fort's parapet. By then, other cannon from nearby forts were joining in, making a "rumbling, deadening sound." As one young Charlestonian recorded in her diary, "the war was on."[7]

More than three thousand shells struck Fort Sumter in the next day and a half. Anderson's men stayed grimly at their posts, hampered by a lack of ammunition and choked by smoke from their big guns and from fires started by enemy shells. In Charleston, civilians climbed to their rooftops to watch the bombardment, cheer the fighting, and await the outcome. The issue was never in doubt. Positioned as they were, the Federal troops had no chance. After thirty-four hours, Anderson surrendered. Despite the heavy shelling, there had been no human fatalities during the battle. Receiving the tattered U.S. flag that had hung over the fort, he and his men were taken out to the relief ship that had remained beyond the harbor during the fight.

Unity and Resolution

As Lincoln had foreseen, the attack on Fort Sumter united and inspired the North to go to war as no argument or persuasion could have done. Citizens rushed to assure him of their support and loyalty. Senators and congressmen called at the White House to offer help in the war effort. Union banners hung from windows, hangmen's nooses proclaiming "Death to Traitors" were suspended from lamp posts, and newspapers wrote fiery editorials expounding their points of view. One editor promised that he would "fight the Secession leaders till Hell froze over, and then fight them on the ice."[8]

Neither side was prepared for war, however, and few people understood the enormity and difficulty of the enterprise they were undertaking. Even army generals,

The First to Die

More than six hundred thousand soldiers died during the four years of the Civil War. The first fatality was Daniel Hough, one of Robert Anderson's men who defended Fort Sumter in 1861. Ironically, Hough's death was accidental and came after the battle ended as historian Bruce Catton describes in *Reflections on the Civil War*.

> Fort Sumter was bombarded for about a day and a half. It returned fire, and all in all, probably 4,000 shells were fired back and forth. At the end of it, Fort Sumter was a wreck. Since the people in the fort were out of food and it was obvious that relieving ships could not come in, Major Anderson surrendered on condition that he and his garrison be transported North, and that he be allowed to fire a final salute to the United States flag when he hauled it down.
>
> A very odd thing then happened. The fighting had gone on for a day and a half, 4,000 shells had been fired, and nobody had been hurt. Twenty-four hours after the fighting had stopped, Anderson gathered his men to board the boats that were to take them North. As he was firing the final salute, a smoldering bit of cloth from one of the cartridges drifted down to the back of the cannon that was firing the salute and touched off a charge of powder. There was an explosion and one soldier was killed. Five more were injured, one of whom eventually died. Two men killed and four men hurt in the great battle of Fort Sumter—all of them after the battle had stopped.

The Confederate flag flies over the ruins of Fort Sumter after its surrender.

many of whom had been trained at the U.S. Military Academy at West Point, had never led large armies into battle before. They would have to gain a knowledge of strategy and tactics through trial and error. Historian Shelby Foote writes, "They'd never been in combat before, most of them, especially on the southern side. So it was just a disorganized, murderous fistfight, a hundred thousand men slamming away at each other. The generals didn't know their jobs, the soldiers didn't know their jobs. It was just pure determination to stand and fight and not retreat."[9]

The determination and ability of men like Confederate general Robert E. Lee (top) and Union general William Tecumseh Sherman (bottom) would be tested by the intensity of the war.

The South benefited from the talents of men such as Robert E. Lee, Thomas "Stonewall" Jackson, and James Ewell Brown "Jeb" Stuart, who seemed to have a genius for fighting and the ability to inspire the men they commanded, but the North's most promising leaders—among them George McClellan, Ambrose Burnside, and Joseph Hooker—found their willingness to fight decreasing as their responsibilities increased. Those who proved most successful in the end—Ulysses S. Grant, George Meade, and William Sherman, to name three—were men of determination, common sense, and ability. They also possessed a certain cold-bloodedness, since the war was one of attrition (a wearing down of the enemy), and winning involved the sacrifice of hundreds of thousands of lives.

The Fortunes of War

Soldiers fought the Civil War in thousands of places across the nation between 1861 and 1865. Men clashed, skirmished, pounded, and sniped at one another in never-to-be-forgotten locales like Bull Run and Gettysburg, and in unremembered spots like Valverde, New Mexico, and Olustee, Florida. Of the multitude of engagements that qualified as battles (large-scale prolonged struggles), both sides won their share. Several of the most momentous or remarkable encounters are included in this book. Fort Sumter marked the beginning of the war; the First Battle of Bull Run (Manassas) awoke Americans to the grim realities of combat. The Battle of the Ironclads was a first in naval warfare; Antietam (Sharpsburg), the bloodiest day of the war. (Northerners often named battles after a nearby geographical feature, while Southerners referred to the nearest town.) Vicksburg addressed the concept of siege; Gettysburg marked the turning point in the fortunes of the South. Whereas the Battle of Cold Harbor was one of Grant's most serious military mistakes, Sherman's March illustrated the effectiveness of "total warfare."

These battles were more than just strategically important; their outcomes reflected the overall fortunes of the

General Ulysses S. Grant in camp. A failure in everything but war and marriage, he would gain fame as one of the military greats of the day.

North and the South as well. Early Confederate victories at Fort Sumter and Bull Run, for instance, affirmed the initial effectiveness of the South's fighting spirit. The Confederate army made do with fewer men and supplies—two men for every three Northerners, 15 percent of the nation's factories, and 33 percent of its farmland—but rank-and-file Confederates were fighting to protect their homes and families from the hated Yankee invaders. Such fervor and desperation tended to even the odds in the first years of the conflict.

Union victories, which became more common as the war progressed—at Gettysburg, Vicksburg, and across Georgia—were a result of the South's waning strength as well as the growing expertise of Union leaders, who had learned what was needed to achieve victory. Men had finally been found who could, in Lincoln's words, "face the arithmetic"[10] (cope with the numbers of lives that had to be sacrificed), and their determination helped the North persevere until the South was crushed and the Union secured.

Victory and Defeat

The appointment of Ulysses S. Grant as commander of all Union armies, in March 1864, marked the beginning of the war's last brutal year, and Union victory was announced in April 1865 at Appomattox Court House, Virginia.

The cost of the struggle proved to be almost immeasurable. A total of more

Dead soldiers lay where they fell at Gettysburg. Over six hundred thousand Americans lost their lives in the Civil War.

the end of their days. Billions of dollars worth of property was destroyed. The Southern economy was crippled and remained so for decades. Railroad systems were wrecked, mills and factories sat vacant, and the Confederate monetary system collapsed with all the attending complications of bank closures and bankruptcy. The South as a whole bore the ultimate humiliation of defeat for generations to come.

No one dreamed of such defeat when Confederates first clashed with Union forces near Manassas, Virginia, in July 1861. The First Battle of Bull Run was Union general Irvin McDowell's chance to prove that he could bring a quick end to the conflict. Instead, he suffered a mortifying reverse, and the nation learned its first painful lesson about war and the price men pay when they take up arms against their brothers.

than six hundred thousand Americans lost their lives in the course of four years, and hundreds of thousands more lived with lost limbs and psychological scars to

First Battle of Bull Run

After the fall of Fort Sumter in April 1861, two months passed as the nation prepared for war. Both North and South put out a call for troops, young men hurried to sign up, and military officials rushed to round up the necessary maps, weapons, uniforms, and other vital war matériel that no one had thought to stockpile before. Politicians made enthusiastic predictions and promises, and citizens took part in torchlight marches that signified support for their respective causes.

Lincoln declared a blockade of Southern ports, directed that suspected Confederate sympathizers be arrested and held without trial, and seized control of telegraph offices to ensure that no subversive messages were wired to the enemy. Jefferson Davis struggled to lead his contentious new government, taking time out to appoint generals to head the fast-growing Confederate army. Slaves in growing numbers began slipping away to the North. Although the Fugitive Slave Act of 1850 decreed that they be returned to their masters, Northerners defiantly dubbed them "contraband of war" (goods seized during a war) and refused to hand them back to owners who had renounced their loyalty to the United States.

An Army of Green Recruits

Serious fighting was not far off, however. After Fort Sumter's fall, Confederates began amassing in Virginia, not far from Washington, and by early summer, thousands of men in gray were camped across the Potomac River from the Capitol, preparing to attack when circumstances were judged to be right.

Near the end of April, large numbers of men from various Northern states began arriving in Washington as well. They spent their days marching and drilling under the command of General Irvin McDowell, a conscientious military man who

Strategic Battles of the Civil War

GETTYSBURG
July 1–3, 1863

Pennsylvania

Ohio

New Jersey

Delaware

ANTIETAM
September 17, 1862

Washington, DC

Maryland

Illinois

Indiana

FREDERICKSBURG
December 13, 1882

West Virginia

Virginia

BULL RUN
1st battle, July 21, 1861
2nd battle,
August 29–30, 1862

Kentucky

Missouri

North Carolina

COLD HARBOR
June 3–7, 1864

Tennessee

Atlantic Ocean

Arkansas

South Carolina

Georgia

Union State

Confederate State

Strategic Battle

FORT SUMTER
April 12–14, 1861

Alabama

Mississippi

VICKSBURG
July 3, 1863

drank no coffee, tea, or spirits and did not smoke or chew tobacco. He was especially proud that when he had once been thrown from a horse and knocked unconscious, he had managed to keep his jaws locked, preventing the doctor from pouring a restorative shot of brandy down his throat.

McDowell was not only straitlaced, he was methodical, and he believed it would take months to turn thousands of farmers, merchants, mountain men, and schoolboys into an efficient, well-disciplined fighting machine. "This is not an army," he warned Lincoln when the president urged

him to go after the enemy. "It will take a long time to make an army."[11] Lincoln could not grant McDowell that time. Troops had been asked to enlist for only three months, and much of that time had already expired. "You are green, it is true," the president responded, "but they [Confederate troops] are green, also; you are all green alike."[12] He told the general to get on with the war, and McDowell obligingly came up with a plan.

On July 16, 1861, he and his thirty-five-thousand-man force set out for Manassas, Virginia, a railroad junction twenty-five miles southwest of Washington, D.C. Their ultimate goal was to end the war by capturing Richmond, less than one hundred miles to the south, but McDowell believed that if he could take control of the railroad that ran between Manassas and Richmond, he would be in a stronger position to move on the Confederate capital. The railroad was behind enemy lines, however, and McDowell would have to break through Confederate general Pierre G. T. Beauregard's twenty-two thousand troops if he wanted to possess it. Beauregard, a capable—and stylish—military man from Louisiana, had been appointed commander of Confederate forces in northeastern Virginia shortly after the fall of Fort Sumter.

As McDowell had observed, his men were neither well disciplined nor battle ready. When they got tired and hungry on the march, they discarded the heavy cartridge boxes that held the ammunition they would use in battle and ate up the rations intended to see them through the fight. "They stopped every moment to pick blackberries or get water, they would not keep in the ranks, order as much as you pleased. . . . They were not used to denying themselves much; they were not used to journeys on foot,"[13] McDowell noted in frustration. As the long blue columns moved on, the men were sometimes commanded to march briskly, sometimes told to stand and wait for reasons that were never explained. Unused to army discipline, they complained loudly. Some wandered off to sit in the shade or to find water, then had to run to

catch up when their column began moving again. In such a disorganized fashion, it took two and one half days to make a twenty-five-mile trip. Later in the war, battle-hardened troops would cover that distance in half the time.

Despite such handicaps, McDowell managed to get his men as far as Centerville, a few miles north of Manassas, by Friday, July 19. There they settled down to await orders and discuss how they were going to whip the Rebs (or Rebels, another term for Confederates). Thus far, the war was proving to be a once-in-a-lifetime adventure, and despite the frustrations, most were enjoying it to its fullest. One man wrote, "Our regiment stacked arms in a large meadow. Rail fences were plenty and we soon had fires burning and coffee cooking in our cups. . . . I enjoyed the evening by the fire and speculating on what might happen on the morrow."[14]

On the other side of Bull Run Creek—a steep-banked stream, deep in places, that threaded its way through the countryside—Beauregard's men undoubtedly did the same. Their leader, however, had already realized that he faced a force larger than his own and wired the Confederate government for backup troops, specifically General Joseph E. Johnston's force, which was stationed in the Shenandoah Valley to the east. Johnston set out with eight thousand men and, by using the Manassas Gap Railroad, was able to get most of them to Bull Run for the battle, although some marched directly from the cars onto the battlefield itself.

Life in Uniform

Many men joined the army believing that soldiering would be more exciting than working in a store or on a farm. Some were seriously disillusioned when they faced the rigor and routine of military life. Historian Shelby Foote describes what life was like for the enlisted man in Geoffrey Ward's *The Civil War, An Illustrated History*.

> It was tough. There were the little things. They made regular twenty-five-mile marches. . . . They made them frequently, and when you were issued a pair of shoes in the northern army, they weren't left foot and right foot, they were the same foot. You *wore* them into be-

ing a left-foot shoe or a right-foot shoe. And when you imagine making twenty-five-mile marches with inferior footwear, let alone barefoot, the way many Confederates were, it's unbelievable the way they could function.

There was a lot of boredom, as there is in all armies. Combat is a very small part of army service if you're talking about the amount of time spent in it. Everything is boring. The food is bad. The time on your hands is bad. The lack of reading materials is bad. It's nearly all boredom. All armies have that saying, "Hurry up and wait." There was an awful lot of that. The boredom was especially oppressive when combined with the heat of summer, as at [the siege of] Vicksburg or Petersburg. Partly out of bravado but mainly out of boredom, the men would leap up on the parapets and make insulting gestures toward the other side while they shot at him—just from sheer boredom. Some of them got shot doing it, too.

Union soldiers at rest during one of their regular twenty-five-mile-long marches.

It was the first time in history that steam-propelled locomotives were used to transport troops in war.

A Gallant Effort

McDowell did not move to strike the enemy until Sunday, July 21, after his men's ammunition and rations were replenished and the enemy's position and strength were carefully noted. To avoid the burning heat of the day, he issued orders for troops to begin moving forward at 3:00 A.M., but the green Federals found marching in the dark difficult. It was after nine o'clock before they crossed Bull Run. Nevertheless, many of them sang

The First Battle of Bull Run was the first time that steam-propelled locomotives were used to transport troops into combat.

and joked as they splashed across the creek at several of its fords, water squelching from their shoes and the sounds of their own artillery already booming above their heads and into the woods beyond. The battle scene was so close to the Capitol that some congressmen and members of Washington society along with their wives and girlfriends rode out to view the fight, and this lent a kind of picnic atmosphere to the day. "We thought it wasn't a bad idea to have the great men from Washington come out to see us thrash the Rebs,"[15] one soldier said.

Warned by his lookouts that the Yankees (the Confederate name for Federal, or Union, troops) were coming from the left, Beauregard realized that he had poorly positioned his troops along the creek. There were too few available to withstand the attack. "My heart for a moment failed me,"[16] he said, then he issued orders to bring in several companies as

quickly as possible. Meanwhile, already entrenched Confederates opened fire on the advancing Federals. One Union man remembered, "We were saluted by a volley of musketry, which, however, was fired so high that all the bullets went over our heads. . . . My first sensation was . . . astonishment at the peculiar *whir* of the bullets, and that the Regiment immediately laid down without waiting for orders."[17]

The fight was on. It was a clumsy, uncoordinated effort, since no one had ever taken part in such a battle before, but the inexperienced troops fought bravely and furiously for hours, hampered by thirst, heavy uniforms, and a baking sun. Guns thundered, smoke billowed, and men fought for position, stumbling over the dead who fell all around them. On a slope near the rear, the onlookers waved their hats and handkerchiefs and shouted encouragement.

By late morning, the Confederates were falling back. Some, so horrified by the deafening racket and chaos all around, ran panic-stricken from the field. "[We] fired a volley and saw the Rebels running," one Massachusetts man said.

"The boys were saying constantly, in great glee, 'We've whipped them.' 'We'll hang Jeff Davis to a sour apple tree.' 'They are running.' 'The war is over.'"[18]

Confederate general Bernard Bee, fated to be killed later that day, managed to check his men's flight when he pointed to General Thomas J. Jackson and his hard-fighting Virginia brigade, which had taken a dramatic stand on a nearby ridge. "Look! There stands Jackson like a stone wall! Rally behind the Virginians."[19] Bee's men steadied and held their lines, while Jackson's nickname stuck and would characterize the fearless, fanatical general for all time.

The First Battle of Bull Run ended in a massive Union retreat called "the great skedaddle." The defeat killed Northern hopes for a quick end to the war.

"The Great Skedaddle"

Around one o'clock, the Federals temporarily halted their assault in order to catch their breath, quench their burning thirst, and reorganize for a new attack. The day seemed to be going well, McDowell thought. He directed that the good news be wired to Lincoln who had been waiting nervously back in Washington. The president relaxed when he got the telegram, confident from McDowell's report that the battle was won.

The Confederates were not beaten, however, and would not be that day. Using the intermission to bring up badly needed reinforcements, they rejoined the battle with new men and renewed energy. Exhausted after a sleepless night and an all-day battle, the Federals continued to fight determinedly, sometimes gaining ground, sometimes losing it, but they had begun to think that the war was more than they had bargained for. Then, about four o'clock, Beauregard ordered a massive counterattack, Stonewall Jackson urged his men to "yell like furies"[20] and, for the first time in history, the eerie, high-pitched rebel yell split the air.

The worn-out Federals lost their nerve. They broke and ran for the rear, and "this [run] soon degenerated still further into a panic,"[21] McDowell later recounted. Bull Run Creek lay between them and safety, and they plunged into it, some drowning in their attempt to get across. "Such a rout I never witnessed before," one officer remembered. "No efforts could induce a single regiment to form after the retreat was commenced."[22]

Seeing the frightened troops rushing toward them, the multitude of onlookers panicked, jumped into their buggies, and whipped up their horses for Washington. The road became jammed, and the crowd turned into a mob, with dust billowing, men cursing, and women screaming. "We found . . . parasols and dainty shawls lost in their flight by the frail, fair ones who had seats in most of the carriages of this excursion,"[23] remembered one Confederate officer who later inspected the field.

The retreat was called "the great skedaddle," and the road back to Washington lay littered with guns, haversacks, blankets, canteens, clothing, and other property that was dropped in the panicky flight. Sometime during the evening it began to rain. The demoralized troops continued to trudge doggedly along the muddy roads, intent upon putting as much distance between the war and themselves as they possibly could. "I saw a steady stream of men, covered with mud, soaked through with rain, who were pouring irregularly . . . up Pennsylvania Avenue toward the Capitol," reported one observer in Washington. "A dense stream of vapor rose from the multitude; but looking closely . . . I perceived they belonged to different regiments, New Yorkers, Michiganders, Rhode Islanders, Massachusettsers, Minnesotians, mingled pell-mell together."[24]

When one soldier was asked if the whole army had gone down to defeat, he answered, "That's more than I know. I know I'm going home. I've had enough fighting to last my lifetime."[25]

The Rebel Yell

The rebel yell reportedly originated at the First Battle of Bull Run (Manassas) as Thomas "Stonewall" Jackson's men charged into wavering Federal ranks. The sound seemed to be confined to the battlefield; Confederate veterans were reluctant to reproduce it for listeners after the war; and thus, according to historian Shelby Foote, "it perished from the sound waves." Foote does his best to describe the yell in Geoffrey Ward's *The Civil War, An Illustrated History*.

They both had a particular way of yelling. The Northern troops made a sort of Hurrah—it was called by one soldier "the deep generous manly shout of the Northern soldier." The Confederates of course had what was called the Rebel Yell. We don't really know what that sounded like. It was basically . . . a sort of fox-hunt yip mixed up with a sort of banshee squall [a shrill ghostly wail], and it was used on the attack. An old Confederate veteran after the war was asked at a United Veterans of the Confederacy meeting in Tennessee somewhere to give the Rebel Yell. The ladies had never heard it. And he said, "It can't be done, except at a run, and I couldn't do it anyhow with a mouthful of false teeth and a stomach full of food." So they never got to hear what it sounded like!

Untested Courage

No enlisted man had an idea of what the fighting would be like before the Civil War, since no one from either side had ever been in a war before. Despite their inexperience, thousands acquitted themselves manfully throughout the grim Battle of Bull Run. Historian Bruce Catton explains in *This Hallowed Ground.*

> There is an unreal quality to most accounts of this battle because they tend to describe it in terms of later battles which were fought after generals and soldiers had learned their trade, and it was not like those battles at all. Nothing went the way it had been planned, except for that first clumsy lunge around the Confederate left. After that, for Northerners and Southerners alike, it was simply a matter of pushing raw troops up to the firing line and hoping for the best.
>
> The men stood up to it better than anyone had a right to expect. A good many of them lost heart and hid in the woods on the way up to the firing line, and a good many more ran away at the first shock, but that happened in every battle all through the war; even with veteran regiments; the amazing thing about Bull Run is that so many of these untested holiday soldiers dug in their heels and fought with great courage. They knew so little about their business that men in the front rank were on occasion shot by their own comrades farther in the rear. . . . Although a great deal was said afterward about the disgraceful rout at Bull Run, the simple fact is that for most of the day the soldiers stood up manfully under a great deal of pounding.

Many untested soldiers fought with great courage at Bull Run, some to the death.

The Victors

The Confederates, too, had stopped fighting, but they were celebrating their victory. Confederate president Jefferson Davis, who, drawn by his love for the military, had been unable to stay away, had arrived in the middle of the afternoon. He recognized the value of a Confederate push into Washington while Northern troops were weak and disorganized, and he asked Beauregard how many men were pursuing the Federals. Beauregard replied that his men were exhausted and hungry and needed rest. Jeb Stuart and his highly mobile cavalrymen were rounding up Union stragglers, and had too many prisoners to take part in any chase. Stonewall Jackson, who had, in fact, stated after the battle, "Give me ten thousand men and I would be in Washington tomorrow,"[26] was slightly wounded and did not have that many troops at his disposal anyway.

If they had been asked, the gray-clad veterans of Bull Run would have rebelled at the thought of marching to Washington. They knew that they had driven the Yankees from the field. They would learn they had killed, wounded, and taken prisoner more than three thousand men (compared to their own two thousand casualties), captured numerous pieces of Federal artillery, half a million rounds of small arms ammunition, and hundreds of muskets. All this proved to them that the battle—and the war—had been won. This belief was so prevalent that those men who were on their way to join up, cursed their bad luck. One later wrote, "We felt that the war was over, and that we would have to return home without even seeing a Yankee soldier. . . . The battle was over and we [were] left out."[27]

Myths Dispelled

While Southerners celebrated their victory and were lulled into underestimating their enemy's fighting potential, Northerners were replacing the myth of a ninety-day war with the realization that the nation faced a long, painful struggle. Soldiers and civilians now had a glimmer of the sacrifice they would have to make, and the physical pain and suffering they would have to endure, if they wanted to win.

The hideousness of that suffering was an eye-opening experience for the men, North and South. Most had pictured the war as a colorful pageant where they could fight but not be wounded, or if they did, the wounds would be clean and neat and painless. In fact, soft lead bullets and exploding shells were particularly messy,

The deaths and injuries at the First Battle of Bull Run brought home the gruesome realities of war.

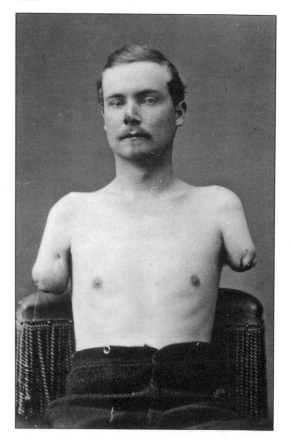

shattering bones, tearing flesh, and producing the goriest of wounds imaginable. Men died painful, lingering deaths during and after every battle, and dirt and neglect contributed to infections and gangrene that claimed even more lives.

The reality of injuries—the ugliness, agony, and death that surrounded them—stunned everyone. Soldiers often vomited when they witnessed the wounded for the first time. "What a horrible sight it was! Here a man, grasping his musket firmly in his hands, stone dead; several with distorted features, all horribly dirty. Many were terribly wounded, some with legs shot off; others with arms gone,"[28] wrote one Union man.

Bull Run also put to rest the myth that the other side was somehow inferior in its fighting ability, that one Rebel could beat ten Yankees or vice versa. In reality, both sides realized that the enemy was made up of gallant warriors, willing to stand and fight against terrible odds. In the words of Bruce Catton, "The boys were a little withdrawn. They weren't quite so bubbly. The first battle had shaken them down very much. After that, you never heard them talk about being impatient to get into action. Any troops who talked that way were fresh from training camp."[29]

Moving On

The news of the Union army's defeat at Bull Run quickly made its way through the North and then across the Atlantic to Europe, bringing with it shock, disbelief, and then gloom. "Today will be known as BLACK MONDAY,"[30] George Templeton Strong, a New York lawyer wrote in his journal. The London *Times* stated, "So short lived has been the American Union that men who saw its rise may live to see its fall." "On every brow sits sullen, scorching, black despair,"[31] wrote Horace Greeley, editor of the *New York Tribune*. Although he had supported the war thus far, Greeley now changed his mind and wrote, "If it is best for the country and for mankind that we make peace with the rebels, and on their own terms, do not shrink even from that."[32]

Lincoln had no intention of compromising, however. Although shaken, he was still committed to saving the Union, and he quickly put out a call for one hundred thousand volunteers, to serve for three years rather than three months. He also decided to replace McDowell with a commander who could inspire men to fight zealously in the days ahead. Lincoln had in mind George B. McClellan, head of the Department of the Ohio, who was highly popular with his men and had won a series of minor battles against the Confederates in western Virginia that spring. Handsome, charismatic, and confident, McClellan had been hailed by the newspapers as a "Young Napoleon," and seemed just the man to lead the Union to victory. The day after Bull Run, Lincoln sent him an urgent telegram: "Circumstances make your presence here necessary. . . . Come hither without delay."[33]

Chapter 2

Battle of the Ironclads

he most famous clashes of the Civil War were usually land battles, struggles for territory or to weaken or kill the enemy. However, one battle that captured the interest of the nation and the world took place on the water, in a natural channel called Hampton Roads, where the Nansemond, James, and Elizabeth Rivers meet off the coast of Virginia.

The Blockade

When the war began, Lincoln recognized the significance of outside support to the Confederate states. His blockade of Southern ports was designed to cut off the supply of European imports, particularly manufactured goods that could be used in the war, as well as to prevent tons of cotton—the mainstay of the Southern economy—from being exported to England.

Blockading ports would accomplish little if thousands of miles of southern coastline, broken by endless inlets and rivers, were not guarded as well. At the beginning of the war, the Federal navy had fewer than fifty vessels to do that job. Under the supervision of Secretary of the Navy Gideon Welles, scores of ships that could help maintain the blockade were purchased or built. By 1862, the southern coast was patrolled by more than four hundred vessels of various kinds. As had been the tradition since the beginning of time, most of these vessels were sailing ships (although some were equipped with coal-powered steam engines), and all were made of wood.

Enter the *Virginia*

There were at least five vessels enforcing the Union blockade in Hampton Roads on March 8, 1862, when there occurred an event that would make naval history. As the crews aboard the *Minnesota*, the *Roanoke*, the *St. Lawrence*, the *Congress*, and the *Cumberland* went about the mundane

Wooden sailing ships like this one were used by the Union navy to blockade Confederate ports at the beginning of the Civil War.

chores that made up their week—it was washday and the riggings were hung with drying clothes—an unidentified cloud of black smoke appeared on the horizon. Curious, the men cleared the decks and stood by on alert. All had heard rumors that the Confederates were building a new kind of warship. If this was it, they were eager to see what it looked like and how it stood up to combat with some of the best conventional warships in the world.

Slowly, ponderously, the stranger came chugging into view. It was the steamship *Virginia*, a four-thousand-ton monstrosity, clad in armor, that its designers hoped would prove to be the attack dog of the Confederate navy. "I regard the possession of an iron-armored ship as a matter of the first necessity,"[34] Confederate secretary of the navy Stephen R. Mallory wrote on May 10, 1861, and by the end of the year he was busy putting together a small fleet of ironclads for the South. The *Virginia*, one of the first of these ships, had originally been the USS *Merrimack*, a wooden-hulled steam frigate (a high-speed, medium-sized war vessel) that the Union had scuttled when it abandoned its Gosport Navy Yard near Norfolk, Virginia, in the spring of 1861. Confederate engineers had raised, rebuilt, and renamed it, and now it looked like no other ship that had ever existed before.

Although it extended almost twenty-three feet under water, the *Virginia's* slanted sides rose just seven feet above the waterline. The ship was covered with two-inch-thick armor plating, designed to deflect the heaviest cannonballs, and housed ten enormous guns mounted fore, aft, and down both sides. A four-foot-long iron ram was attached to the vessel's prow for piercing the wooden hulls of its more vulnerable enemies. Black, ugly, and awkward, the *Virginia* was compared by some to a huge, half-submerged crocodile,

Life on the Water

Never as powerful as the army, the navy nevertheless became an important arm of the military during the Civil War. Thousands of men, black and white, served on board a variety of vessels that ranged from ferryboats to frigates, tugs to ironclads. Life on the water was unique, sometimes dangerous, and always hard work as Geoffrey Ward describes in *The Civil War, An Illustrated History*.

Life aboard ship was rugged and monotonous. An officer suggested that his mother would have some inkling of what blockade duty was like if she would "go to the roof on a hot summer day, talk to a half-dozen degenerates, descend to the basement, drink tepid water full of iron rust, climb to the roof again, and repeat the process until . . . fagged [tired] out, then go to bed with everything shut tight."

Crews included old salts, immigrants who spoke no English, country boys who'd never seen the ocean before, let alone sailed on it. Blacks served at sea long before they were allowed to fight on land, but only in the lowest ranks. Each day was devoted to scrubbing, painting, drilling, repairing, coaling, target practice—day after day, week after week. Food was often limited to two dishes: pickled beef and "dogs' bodies"—dried peas, boiled in a cloth. Too many weeks at sea produced a condition one naval surgeon called "*land* sickness"—a morbid longing to go ashore.

The crew of a Union vessel gathers on deck. A black sailor tries to ease the monotony of life on board by playing a banjo.

whereas others described it as "a huge terrapin [turtle] with a large round chimney about the middle of its back."[35] Those men who had seen river floods claimed it looked like a barn that had sunk to its eaves and was drifting downstream.

The *Virginia* had faults other than ugliness. It was enormously heavy and sat so low in the water that it could only move in deep water channels. It was incredibly slow, and as "unwieldy as Noah's ark."[36] Its crew needed more than thirty minutes to turn around in calm water, longer when a wind was blowing. The ship's engines, which had been immersed in salt water for months prior to the overhaul, were old, wheezy, and unpredictable; the dark interior was cramped and airless. Those who peered inside predicted it would become "an enormous metallic burial-case"[37] for the three-hundred-man crew.

An Unequal Fight

The *Virginia*'s captain, Commodore Franklin Buchanan, sixty-two-year-old former superintendent of Annapolis Naval Academy, focused on the strengths of his unique new warship and was anxious to see what it could achieve in battle. Buchanan was a veteran sailor who had joined the navy as a midshipman at the age of fifteen. He was tall, white haired, and harsh featured, with piercing eyes and a brisk step that never faltered or stumbled even on the pitching deck of a ship. Intensely loyal to his native state of Maryland, he assumed it would join the Confederacy at the beginning of the war. He had had to make the best of his mistaken decision to support the South when Maryland remained in the Union.

Buchanan was in command when the *Virginia* steamed downriver on what was supposed to be a trial run on March 8. Although the ship's guns had never been fired, and workmen were still making last-minute adjustments on deck, when Buchanan saw Union warships lying at anchor just ahead, he could not resist the temptation to attack. Boldly he directed his vessel into Hampton Roads and headed left up the James River, past the *Congress* and straight for the *Cumberland*.

Recognizing danger, the *Congress* was the first to fire on the ironclad, giving it a full broadside blast that made hardly a dent in the metal plates that sheathed it. The ironclad returned fire, killing and wounding several sailors. It then chugged

"Old Buck"

Determining where one's loyalty lay at the war's beginning was a difficult task and often ended friendships and divided families. Such was the case for Captain Franklin "Old Buck" Buchanan of Maryland, commander of the *Virginia*. Naval historian A. A. Hoehling explains in *Thunder at Hampton Roads*.

In 1861 Buchanan was commandant of the important Washington Navy Yard. And then he made his wrong guess: that his beloved Free State would secede. He resigned his commission—and as quickly asked [U.S. Secretary of the Navy] Gideon Welles to reinstate him when it was apparent that Maryland, if a bit shaky . . . would persevere under Old Glory. The navy secretary bluntly informed the senior officer that the service did not need irresolute commanders.

Old Buck became emotional. He remonstrated that it was extremists who had "ruined our glorious country" and that he would be "miserable" out of the United States Navy. Welles was content to allow him to remain in such an unhappy state.

As it turned out, Buchanan became bitter, undergoing what some interpreted as a sort of personality change. Before long he went so far as to refer to his erstwhile [former] shipmates as "vile vagabonds"! All of this was especially distressing to his older brother (by two years), McKean, inspector of provisions at Boston Navy Yard, who did *not* believe his allegiance was first to Maryland.

on toward the *Cumberland*, blasting it with a shell, "spraying jagged splinters all about, and . . . killing nine Marines."[38] The *Cumberland* also returned fire, but its shots bounced off the side of the ironclad "like India rubber balls,"[39] as one officer later described. Boldly, Buchanan closed on the larger ship, punching a hole in its side with his metal ram, which broke off as the ironclad swung clear. With the seas pouring in, the *Cumberland* began to go down. Its crew bravely kept firing as long as their guns remained above water, but the ship finally sank with only its flag, flying from the mainmast, still visible above the waves.

Victorious, the *Virginia* ponderously turned in preparation for its next on-

slaught. The captain of the *Congress* recognized his own danger, spread his sails, and promptly ran aground in the confinement of the channel. Buchanan finished his turn and ordered his crew to open fire. The *Congress*'s crew defended itself as best it could, but shells hit the Union vessel with such deadly effect that, as historian Shelby Foote writes, "her captain dead and her scuppers [deck-level openings for drainage] running red with blood, a lieutenant ran up the white flag of surrender."[40] In the exchange Buchanan was also injured, and command of the *Virginia* passed to executive officer Lieutenant Catesby R. Jones.

Jones made short work of the Union warship, blasting it with red-hot cannonballs that set fire to everything they struck. Franklin Buchanan's brother, McKean, whose loyalties lay with the North, was a temporary member of the crew onboard the *Congress*, and died in the fire.

While all this had been happening, the *St. Lawrence* and the *Minnesota* were doing their best to get into the fight. (The *Roanoke* had a broken propeller shaft and sat helpless throughout the battle.) Angling into position during the ebb tide, however, both ran aground in the shallow water of the channel.

The Cumberland *(left) sinks after being attacked by the* Virginia *(right). The crew of the Union ship continued firing their cannons until the guns were under water.*

Jones recognized that his ship could face the same fate and moved off into the mouth of the Elizabeth River for the night. There, he unloaded his wounded (two men had been killed and some two dozen injured) and checked for damages.

These were considerable but not serious. The *Virginia*'s iron ram was gone, two guns had been damaged, and nonessentials such as an anchor, a smokestack, and some railings had been lost. But the vital armor plates remained intact and uncracked, the steering mechanism was undamaged, and the engines still worked as well as they ever had. That night, the ironclad's crew, too excited over their victory to sleep, watched the *Congress* burn and cheered when its powder magazine exploded shortly after midnight. They looked forward to the next day, when they would finish off the rest of the Union warships that lay stranded across the channel.

Enter the *Monitor*

The events of March 8 were quickly wired to Washington, informing Lincoln and his cabinet that the Confederates now had an indestructible "floating battery" that had destroyed two warships and would surely attack three more as soon as the sun rose. Horrified, Secretary of War Edwin M. Stanton predicted that the *Virginia* would change the entire course of the war. "She will destroy . . . every naval vessel; she will lay all the cities on the seaboard under contribution. . . . Not unlikely, we shall have a

shell or a cannonball from one of her guns in the White House before we leave this room,"[41] he cried.

Secretary of the Navy Welles saw the situation from a calmer perspective. He reminded Stanton that the *Virginia* reportedly drew too much water to get up the Potomac within shelling distance of the Capitol. He also reminded everyone that the Union had a secret weapon of its own that could even the balance of power. Having heard rumors that the South was constructing an ironclad warship, the Federal navy had taken similar steps in order to be prepared. By coincidence, the newly completed Union ironclad, the *Monitor*, had set out for Hampton Roads several days before. In fact, it was scheduled to arrive there about the time the cabinet meeting was taking place.

The *Monitor* was indeed in Hampton Roads, but it did not get there without trouble. It had been designed by cranky, Swedish-born John Ericsson, a rugged sixty-year-old inventor who lived for his work and was as temperamental as he was talented. He had long dreamed of building a warship for the navy, so when he heard that the Union wanted an ironclad, he dug out a scale model prototype that he had conceived seven years earlier and promptly submitted it for consideration. "The sea shall ride over her and she shall live in it like a duck,"[42] he vowed when skeptics suggested that his creation was unstable.

The *Monitor* had left New York in a snowstorm, then instantly fallen victim to design shortcomings that jeopardized the passage. "We ran first to the New York side and then to Brooklyn & so back and forth across the [East] river . . . like a drunken man on a sidewalk. . . . We found she would not answer her rudder at all,"[43] remembered one of the crew. Once at sea, freezing waves flooded the hold, pumps proved inadequate, the ship filled with gas from the coal-burning furnace when ventilator fans failed, and some of the crew were rendered unconscious. Nevertheless, the *Monitor* survived the trip, just as Ericsson had promised it would.

Like the *Virginia*, the *Monitor* was an ugly craft, built to attack and to withstand attack rather than impress bystanders with its graceful lines. Some called it "a tin can on a shingle"; others dubbed it "a cheese-box on a raft."[44] Its deck was only a foot or two above the waterline, and it had only two guns, but these were eleven-inch reinforced cannon and were housed in a revolving turret amid ship, designed to be pointed in any direction.

More heavily reinforced than the *Virginia*, the *Monitor* carried armor up to nine inches thick but was lighter and easier to

The Union ironclad Monitor, *also called "a cheese-box on a raft," steams briskly ahead in calm seas. During rough weather, waves would break over the hull and flood the hold.*

turn than its opponent. Thus it was able to maneuver in tighter places and shallower waters. For the comfort of its crew, all of whom were experienced naval shipmen, Ericsson had designed forced-air ventilation and a compressed-air flush toilet.

Its captain, Lieutenant John L. Worden, had been the first Northerner captured by the Confederates while delivering secret messages the previous year to a Union squadron stationed in Pensacola, Florida. Worden, forty-four years old, had spent seven months in a prison camp before being exchanged. Ready to strike back at his enemies, he piloted the *Monitor* into Hampton Roads just after midnight on March 9 and silently pulled up alongside the *Minnesota*. In his opinion, it was the vessel most vulnerable to the *Virginia*'s attack the next morning. Therefore he would be there to protect it.

Iron Against Iron

At 7:30 A.M. on March 9, the *Virginia* again appeared, puffing slowly but steadily toward the stranded *Minnesota*. Worden was prepared and steamed forward out of the shadows into the open water at the enemy's approach.

The sudden appearance of this unlooked for vessel surprised everyone on the *Virginia*. "We thought at first it was a raft on which one of the *Minnesota*'s boilers was being taken to shore for repairs," one of the crew said, "and when suddenly a shot was fired from her turret we imagined an accidental explosion of some kind had taken place on the raft."[45] Surprise was soon translated into action, however. The *Virginia* fired a blast at the newcomer that would have wreaked havoc with a wooden vessel. The shells struck the *Monitor*'s turret and bounced harmlessly away. The Federal ironclad swung her two guns into position and returned fire. The balls had an equally negligible effect on the *Virginia*.

Yesterday's fight had been an unequal clash of iron against wood, but this day it was iron against iron. It was the first battle between ironclad vessels anywhere in the world, and the two ships proved to be well matched. The fight lasted four hours, and both pounded each other mercilessly.

It was hot, dirty, deafening business. "My men and myself were perfectly black with smoke and powder," reported one officer on the *Monitor*. "My nerves and muscles twitched as though electric shocks were continually passing through them, and my head ached as if it would burst. . . . I thought my brain would come

In the first ever battle between ironclads, the Virginia *(left) and the* Monitor *exchange fire. The Union ship used its speed and steering ability to outmaneuver the Confederate vessel.*

right out over my eyebrows."[46] Standing by their guns, both crews quickly learned not to touch the bulkheads, since a shot hitting the outside of the vessel could kill or seriously injure a man inside. One of the *Monitor*'s crew, resting his knee against the turret wall, was knocked unconscious when a shell struck. The heads of bolts and screws that came loose and flew around the *Monitor*'s interior every time the *Virginia* scored a direct hit posed another serious threat to the lives of those inside.

The *Monitor* was hampered by its need to protect the still-grounded *Minnesota*, but the Union ironclad's greater speed and ease of steering allowed it to circle its opponent and to maneuver out of the way whenever the *Virginia* tried to use its ramming capacity. The *Virginia* had plenty of brute force, but ramming and shelling failed to break the enemy. Thus Jones, in charge a second day, decided to try a more intrepid approach—blinding the Union crew by throwing tarpaulins over the gunslits in the turret, then boarding the vessel and prying open the hatch.

It was a bold plan, although it would have been foiled by the *Monitor*'s crew, who were equipped with hand grenades to throw if the enemy tried to board. Nevertheless, Worden would not let Jones get within grappling distance. Finally, from only ten yards away, Jones blasted a shell directly at the *Monitor*'s pilot house, hitting the slotted opening through which Worden peered. The direct hit stunned

and partly blinded the Union captain and sprung the iron lid to expose the interior of the ship. Worden retained enough awareness to order a retreat, and the *Monitor* steered off into shallower waters where it could be safe from attack for the moment.

Standoff

While the Union crew got Worden to his cabin and assessed the damage they had suffered, Jones and the *Virginia* calculated their own chances of success if they continued the fight. The ship's stack was so damaged that its fires could not draw properly; consequently their speed was reduced from five miles per hour to less than half that. The pounding the vessel had endured had loosened its seams, and it was settling from the weight of the water it was taking on. In addition, the wound where the iron ram had torn off was leaking.

Taking all things into account, Jones felt it would be prudent to leave well enough alone. His ship was still afloat, and he had inflicted severe damage on his opponent and its captain. Since the *Monitor* had pulled back first, he reasoned that he could declare a Confederate victory and leave the field without further pursuit of the enemy.

The Federals, with no wish to continue the fight either, viewed developments in an entirely different light. They saw the *Virginia*'s withdrawal as an admission of defeat. As the Confederate vessel moved slowly back toward Norfolk, the *Monitor* steamed forward like a victorious fighter. It had saved the *Minnesota*, repelled the *Virginia*, and lived to fight another day. There was no doubt among its crew that they had triumphed over their enemy and driven him from the field.

A New Generation of Warships

For all intents and purposes, the first battle of the ironclads ended in a draw, although both sides claimed victory and historians still debate the ramifications of the contest. All agree, however, that wooden warships were the losers, since they were no longer a match for opponents that neither burned nor broke apart under attack.

By the end of the war, the North was using more than forty ironclads on its coasts and rivers, while the Confederacy had twenty-four. Of these, most in the North were "monitors"—that is, armored, steam-powered vessels built along the lines of the original *Monitor*—whereas Southern ironclads were similar in design to the *Virginia* and were usually referred to as "rams," even though they might lack that capability. Construction of Southern ironclads eventually declined under the negligence of a penniless, preoccupied, Confederate high command, but later Northern ironclads were better designed and stronger than the original. They eventually became a part of Union naval strategy, serving with conventional wooden warships in blockades and in river maneuvers.

The Winner

The debate over who won the first battle of the ironclads began when the guns fell silent at Hampton Roads and has continued ever since. The battle had wide ramifications, particularly for General George McClellan's Peninsula Campaign, since the presence of the *Virginia* would have blocked the landing of McClellan's troops at Fort Monroe. Bruce Catton explains in *Terrible Swift Sword.*

> The battle was over. It had been a complete stand-off, and Assistant Secretary of the Navy Gustavus V. Fox said the most that could be said when he telegraphed [General George] McClellan that night that the battle showed "a slight superiority in favor of the *Monitor*. . . ." *Monitor*'s chief engineer, Alban C. Stimers, was more optimistic, and he telegraphed congratulations to Ericsson, telling him that "you saved this place to the nation by furnishing us with the means to whip an ironclad frigate that was, until our arrival, having it all her own way with our most powerful vessels."
>
> In a way, *Monitor* had won something important; she had at least restored the status quo. As long as she remained afloat, McClellan could bring his army down in transports and put men and supplies ashore near Fort Monroe. The [Union] army's campaign against Richmond could go ahead, even though *Virginia*'s presence would impose certain handicaps. But the weight of the whole campaign rested on this queer, mastless warship with the revolving turret. *Monitor* could not be risked; she could neutralize *Virginia*, but she could do nothing more than that; dared do nothing more, because of all the ships in the United States Navy this was the one that must not be lost.

Because of their resistance to fire and shell, only twelve out of a total of sixty-six ironclads were lost in action during the war. Some were lost after being rammed, or after being struck by naval mines (called torpedoes at the time). The Union ship *Keokuk*, a non-monitor design, and the USS *Cincinnati* were the only vessels to go down as a result of gunfire. The *Cincinnati*, a Union river ironclad, was unique in that it was sunk, raised, and repaired, then sunk again later in the war.

After Hampton Roads, wooden warships were made obsolete by ironclads such as the Union's Onondaga *(pictured). This particular ship had two turrets instead of the* Monitor's *one.*

Inglorious End

Despite their renown, neither the *Monitor* nor the *Virginia* survived to the end of the Civil War. After guarding the Union fleet at Hampton Roads for several months, the Union ironclad was being towed around Cape Hatteras, North Carolina, during a heavy storm in late 1862 when it foundered and went down. One of the rescued crew recorded its demise. "About one o'clock on the morning of Wednesday, December 31st, she sank and we saw her no more."[47] Even earlier than that, the *Virginia*, too unstable to take out into the open sea, had been set afire by her own crew when the Confederates abandoned the Gosport Naval Yards to George McClellan, on his way up the Virginia peninsula in March 1862. One member of the Federal fleet watched her burn. "The casemate [armored enclosure] grew hotter and hotter, until finally it became red-hot, so that we could distinctly mark its outlines, and remained in this condition for fully half an hour, when, with a tremendous explosion, [it] went into the air and was seen no more."[48]

Though the *Monitor* and the *Virginia* were merely awkward prototypes of later sophisticated warships, they were remarkable for the change they brought about in naval warfare. One Southerner described the significance of the *Virginia* to a friend in Europe. "Our 'Virginia' by her performances in Hampton Roads, has, at a single dash, overturned the 'wooden walls' of Old England and rendered effete [obsolete] the navies of the world."[49]

The same could be said of the *Monitor* as well.

Chapter 3

Battle of Antietam

By the summer of 1862, Americans had been at war for more than a year and understood that the conflict was going to be a long one. Southern troops were ragged, footsore, and hungry, but still retained their strong fighting spirit. Union general George B. McClellan, executing his plan to capture Richmond by moving up the Virginia peninsula, was slowly pushing Joseph E. Johnston, commander of Confederate forces in Virginia, back toward the Confederate capital. Around the first of June, Johnston was wounded during the Battle of Fair Oaks (Seven Pines) and was replaced by Robert E. Lee, a Virginian who would rise to be head of all Confederate forces during the war. "The shot that struck me down was the best ever fired for the Confederacy,"[50] Johnston later wrote.

A Distinguished Leader

Robert E. Lee, the son of "Light-Horse Harry" Lee of Revolutionary War fame, was the epitome of a Southern gentleman—gracious, intelligent, honorable, and refined. "Lee is the handsomest man of his age I ever saw," observed a visitor from England. "His manners are most courteous and full of dignity. . . . He has none of the small vices . . . and his bitterest enemy never accused him of any of the greater ones."[51] Distinguished for bravery during his thirty-two years in the U.S. Army, and highly recommended by general in chief of the army Winfield Scott, Lee was Abraham Lincoln's first choice to head up all Union armies in early 1861. The Virginian's loyalty to his home state was strong, however. After much soul-searching he refused Lincoln's offer and shortly thereafter resigned to join the Confederacy.

As head of Virginia's army, Lee was nicknamed "Granny Lee" for a time early in the war after failing to hold western Virginia for the Confederacy. His talents as a general soon became apparent, however, earning him the confidence of Jefferson Davis and the love of his men. Stonewall Jackson, who placed his trust in no one but God Almighty, once remarked, "So great is my confidence in General Lee that I am willing to follow him blindfolded."[52] Lee's military genius helped the Confederacy win battles, but it also extended the length of the war and the devastation wrought against the South. Without the Virginian's talented leadership the Confederate army would not have been able to stand for long against superior Northern forces.

Lee called his new force the Army of Northern Virginia, and in June 1862 he repeatedly attacked McClellan's larger army in a series of clashes known as the Battles of the Seven Days. All but one of the battles could be judged a Union victory, but at their end, McClellan withdrew his troops back to the James River, convinced that he faced imminent defeat.

The needless retreat motivated President Lincoln to transfer McClellan's troops to General John Pope's command, and in late August, Pope clashed with Lee in the Second Battle of Bull Run near Manassas. Union forces were again driven

Union and Confederate troops clash once again at the Second Battle of Bull Run. Despite superior numbers, the North suffered another embarrassing defeat.

from the field. Despite superior numbers, the North had added another embarrassing defeat to its record, and Lincoln again awarded McClellan command of the Army of the Potomac, hoping that he would restore its morale and eventually lead it to victory. "We must use the tools we have,"[53] the president explained to his cabinet.

The War Moves North

Northerners had barely come to grips with the fact that their armies had been defeated a second time at Manassas, when Robert E. Lee decided to carry the war north into Maryland. The commander had three reasons for taking the offensive: his men needed food, shoes, and clothing that were hard to find in the South; Virginia needed a respite after being the scene of some of the most destructive fighting for a year; and Maryland, an undecided border state, might join the Confederacy if it were personally invited by gallant, well-behaved Southern troops.

Lee had other motives for invading the North, as well. Threatening Washington and Baltimore would demonstrate Southern strength and determination and would perhaps motivate Northerners to sue for peace. If not, a victory against the North could gain the South diplomatic recognition from European nations whose support would be invaluable.

When the forty-thousand-man Army of Northern Virginia crossed into Maryland in early September 1862, however,

they did not appear to be a strong and threatening force. Many of the enlisted men were sick from living on green corn; a quarter of them were shoeless. Lee had fallen from his horse a few days before and rode in an ambulance with both hands bandaged and splinted. Stonewall Jackson suffered from an injured back. Two of Lee's best generals, John Bell Hood and A. P. Hill, were under arrest for quarreling with their superiors and rode under guard at the rear of their men. "This body of men moving along with no order, their guns carried in every fashion, no two dressed alike, their officers hardly distinguishable from the privates. . . . Were *these* the men that had driven back again and again our splendid legions?"[54] asked one woman they passed.

Few Marylanders switched loyalties to the South as a result of the march, but Lee followed through with his plan anyway, dividing his forces and sending Stonewall Jackson with twenty-two thousand men to capture the Federal garrison at Harpers Ferry. Lee himself moved the rest of his forces northwest to Hagerstown, where he planned to join up with Jackson, then capture Harrisburg, the capital of Pennsylvania and a key rail center for the Union.

Change of Plan

The plan was sound, but, unexpectedly, George McClellan forced Lee to alter it. "Little Mac," as his men affectionately called him, had reorganized and revitalized the Army of the Potomac in a shorter time than anyone had expected. Now it was in pursuit of Lee, and McClellan had the good fortune of knowing the Virginian's battle plans, which had been found wrapped around three cigars at an abandoned Confederate campsite. "Here is a paper with which, if I cannot whip Bobbie Lee, I will be willing to go home," [55] McClellan exulted.

The young general suffered from doubts and misconceptions that doomed his chances of success, however. He was convinced that Lincoln and General Winfield Scott were foolish, ignorant, and eager to see him fail. Due to erroneous reports from the spies he employed, he believed that Lee's army was twice the size of his own, when in fact it was seldom more than half that size. Thus, in order to avoid disaster, McClellan proceeded slowly and carefully, dotting every "i" and crossing every "t" as he prepared for attack. One of Lee's staff remarked that the Army of Northern Virginia had a single but important advantage when it went into the Battle of Antietam: McClellan brought along superior numbers of forces, but he also brought along himself.

With his plans known, Lee changed strategy and concentrated his scant forces in defensive positions near the town of Sharpsburg, Maryland. By September 16, the two armies sat poised on opposite banks of Antietam Creek, a placid stream, shallow enough to be forded in some places, spanned by several stone bridges.

McClellan, with around ninety thousand men, might have easily beaten Lee if he had attacked promptly, but, always his own worst enemy, he wasted sixteen hours drawing up extensive plans and positioning his men and guns. The hours gave Stonewall Jackson time to rejoin Lee, effectively doubling the Confederate force.

The Cornfield

Thomas "Stonewall" Jackson was a strange combination of religious fanatic and great warrior—a man who prayed as he went into battle, then demanded the impossible from his men and judged it "commendable" for them to be killed in action. (Jackson himself was accidently shot by his own men on May 2, 1863, and died eight days later.) Ironically, his men admired him despite his cold-blooded approach to war, since they gained a reputation for invincibility when under his command. Jackson himself was fearless, even in the hottest fighting, and always knew exactly what he wanted done. "Once you get them running, you stay right on top of them, and that way a small force can defeat a large one every time," [56] he observed.

Jackson had hidden his men in a clump of woods that edged an open cornfield on the morning of September 17 when Union general Joseph Hooker ordered his artillery to begin a heavy assault on the Confederates at about 6:00 A.M. As Jackson's men returned fire, Hooker's troops began to advance, their objective

Civil War Spies

George McClellan's hesitation to fight the enemy stemmed from reports he received from his chief of intelligence Henry Pinkerton, a former railroad detective, later head of the renowned Pinkerton Detective Agency. Pinkerton's estimation of the size of the Confederate army was grossly inaccurate and led indirectly to McClellan's demotion. Information-gathering by other spies during the war, however, proved extremely helpful to military leaders on both sides, as Geoffrey Ward points out in *The Civil War, An Illustrated History*.

> By all odds, the most useful military intelligence either army gathered during the war was provided to Union officers by mostly anonymous slaves and contrabands, eager to help bring about the Confederacy's collapse. . . . But there were more conventional agents at work as well. Even before Bull Run, secrets streamed between Washington and Richmond: Allan Pinkerton ran the Federal Secret Service; Confederate Major William Norris, official head of the Confederate Signal Bureau, oversaw a clandestine spy network that extended as far north as Montreal. . . .
>
> Women made good operatives: they were suspected less quickly than men and, if caught, punished less severely. Perhaps the most celebrated female agent was Belle Boyd, whose admirers called her "La Belle Rebelle." Six highly publicized arrests failed to stop her from soliciting secrets from Union officers in Washington. . . . Perhaps the ablest female operative working for the Union was Elizabeth Van Lew, a Richmond unionist thought a harmless eccentric by her neighbors, who managed to plant a spy among Jefferson Davis's own servants.
>
> For men, spying, desertion, and treating with the enemy were often rewarded with death by hanging or firing squad. In November 1863, a southern courier, Sam Davis, was sentenced to death for spying at Pulaski, Tennessee. His bravery on the scaffold proved so moving that the commanding general could not bring himself to order the trap sprung. Davis finally gave the order himself.

Confederate spy Belle Boyd, also known as "La Belle Rebelle," was one of the more famous female agents of the war.

being the Confederate artillery, which was positioned near a tiny whitewashed church belonging to the Dunkers, a fundamentalist sect that believed even a steeple was frivolous and immodest. The Confederates moved out to meet them, and the volley of shells from both sides destroyed everyone and everything it touched. "Every stalk of corn in the greater part of the field was cut as closely as could have been done with a knife and the slain lay in rows precisely as they had stood in their ranks a few moments before,"[57] Hooker remembered.

Despite the deadly barrage, the Federals made good progress, "loading and firing with demoniacal fury,"[58] in the words of one Wisconsin man. However, Jackson lost no time in sending in reserves: a division of tough Texans who were furious because they were interrupted while preparing breakfast, their first real meal in days. The angry Confederates pushed the Federals back into the cornfield, only to be hit by Union guns that cut down 60 percent of them. Reinforcements from both sides moved in quickly to take the place of the fallen. Author Albert Marrin writes:

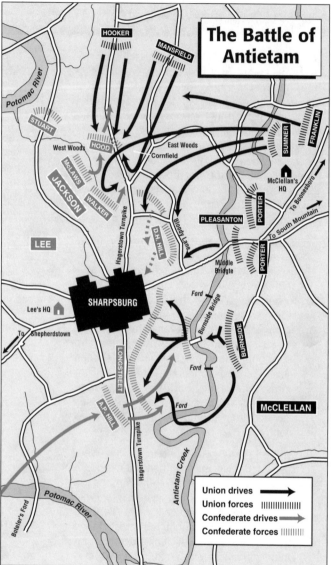

The Battle of Antietam

Union drives
Union forces
Confederate drives
Confederate forces

The cornfield became a slaughter pen. Men lost control, some weeping, some screaming, and some bursting into hysterical laughter. Fighting at close quarters, soldiers went at one another with bayonets and clubbed rifles. They rolled on the ground, punching, biting, choking, scratching. Cannon smoke blanketed the area, covering the sweating men with an oily black film. It was so thick that you could not tell friend from foe a foot away.[59]

The battle lines moved back and forth across the cornfield countless times, with neither side able to establish mastery. By midmorning all were exhausted and pulled back, acknowledging a stalemate. Union losses tallied near seven thousand dead and wounded. Confederate casualties were more than five thousand, but from the outset they had had fewer men to spare. When one Confederate officer who had taken part in the fight was asked where his division was, he replied, "Dead on the field."[60]

Bloody Lane

In midmorning, the struggle shifted south to the center of Lee's forces, where Confederates had taken up positions along a sunken country road, edged by a split-rail fence that ran between two fields. The road served as a perfect rifle pit, so when Union troops raced forward, unaware of the danger they faced, Confederates simply waited for the right moment and cut them down. "The brave Union commander, superbly mounted, placed himself in front, while his band cheered them with martial music," remembered Confederate colonel John B. Gordon, commander of the 6th Alabama. "I thought, 'What a pity to spoil with bullets such a scene of martial beauty!'"[61]

The advancing Federals were hit with a hail of bullets. Those who survived retreated, reformed their lines, and charged a second time. The Confederates again opened fire and the men in blue fell back. Five times the Federals made their assault, suffering terrible casualties and gaining little ground. Finally, after three hours of fierce fighting, a small group of New Yorkers managed to edge to the right and reach a small hill

More than twenty-five hundred Confederates were killed or wounded in this trench at the Battle of Antietam. It would be renamed Bloody Lane as a result of the slaughter.

that overlooked the road. There, they could fire down on the enemy, and suddenly the sunken road became a trap.

The Confederates, huddled together in their trench, were defenseless against an attack from above. "We were shooting them [the Confederates] like sheep in a pen," remembered one Federal. "If a bullet missed the mark at first it was liable to strike the further bank, angle back and take them secondarily."[62] The sunken road—soon renamed Bloody Lane—rapidly filled with bodies, two and three deep. Some Confederates scrambled for safety, but Federals jumped after them into the trench, knelt on the bodies, and cut them down as they attempted to flee. When the bluecoats ran out of ammunition, they seized rifles from the dead under their feet and continued firing. More than twenty-five hundred Confederates were killed or wounded at Bloody Lane. "No tongue can tell, no mind conceive, no pen portray the horrible sights I witnessed this morning," one Pennsylvanian commented. "Of this war I am heartily sick and tired."[63]

Burnside's Bridge

The Confederate line had broken in the middle. The Federals had won the assault on the sunken road, although they paid a high price for their victory—almost three thousand casualties in three hours of fighting. While they fought, Union general Ambrose E. Burnside and his corps of more than twelve thousand men were trying to carry out their part of McClellan's battle plan—get across Antietam Creek and capture the town of Sharpsburg.

Burnside, an honest, likable soldier who would reluctantly replace McClellan in November 1862, lacked the daring and drive to easily accomplish such a challenging task. The bewhiskered general (his name inspired the term *sideburns*) was prone to be nervous and to make poor decisions under pressure. Today, he faced six hundred Georgian sharpshooters, led by Brigadier General Robert A. Toombs (Confederate Secretary of State before he resigned to join the army), and they had him at a disadvantage from the start.

The Georgians had stationed themselves behind trees and boulders on a steep bluff that overlooked the river, and fired down on the Federals every time they dared set foot on the stone bridge that Burnside had elected to use for his crossing. Ironically, the river was shallow enough that Burnside's men could have crossed it at any point, but Burnside was so single-minded that he never considered that option. It was one o'clock before the Federals finally managed to get across the span and three o'clock before they painstakingly reorganized into battle lines and were ready to move again.

Only two thousand Confederates defended Sharpsburg itself, and Burnside's men pushed forward relentlessly until they were on the outskirts of town. Then, when a Union victory seemed inevitable, the unexpected happened. Confederate general

A. P. Hill, who had stayed behind at Harpers Ferry to secure supplies, arrived on the scene. Footsore from their march, the Confederate reinforcements had enough strength left to smash into Burnside's flank, driving him back out of town.

Burnside, who had been promised support from McClellan should he need it, sent a courier pounding off for help. McClellan refused to shift his troops, however. "It would not be prudent,"[64] he said inexplicably. Thus Burnside watched in frustration as his men were pushed back over the ground they had recently taken. They finally dug in near the bridge, for all intents and purposes back where they had begun. Historian Shelby Foote writes, "As night came down, the two armies disengaged, and when the torches of the haystack pyres [fires, set alight by bursting shells] went out, darkness filled the valley of the Antietam, broken only by the lanterns of the medics combing the woods and cornfields for the injured."[65]

Rest and Reevaluation

Back in their tents, Lee and his generals conferred on the best plan for the next day, convinced that McClellan would order another attack. They had suffered terrible losses, and their chances of success

General Burnside's troops charge over the bridge at Antietam, only to be driven back by Confederate reinforcements.

were slim, but Lee was adamant that the battle would go on if the Federals pressed. At his own headquarters, McClellan read a wire from President Lincoln, who had received reports of the day's events and assumed that Little Mac would follow up as well. "God bless you and all with you," Lincoln wrote. "Destroy the rebel army if possible." [66]

McClellan, however, did not choose to fight the next day. "After a night of anxious deliberation and a full and careful survey of the situation and condition of our army . . . I concluded that the success of an attack on the eighteenth was not certain," [67] he later wrote. When morning dawned uneventfully, Lee and his weary troops took the opportunity to retreat safely back across the Potomac River into Virginia. The battle of Antietam was over. "I have heard but one feeling expressed about [Maryland]," wrote a Confederate soldier to his wife, "and that is a regret at our having gone there." [68]

Confederate artillerymen lie dead next to their cannon. The Battle of Antietam was the single bloodiest day of the war.

The Bloodiest Day

Antietam proved to be the bloodiest single day of the Civil War. The Union lost more than two thousand dead and ten thousand wounded or missing. Confederate dead, wounded, and missing totaled more than ten thousand, but that was one-quarter of Lee's entire army.

As was the case after most battles in the Civil War, the task of dealing with the wounded fell to local residents, who were expected to supply aid and shelter until the injured could be conveyed to an urban hospital. Makeshift hospitals were set up in courthouses, churches, schools, and private homes. Near Sharpsburg, one farmer's wife recalled, "The wounded filled every building and overflowed into the country round, into farm-houses, barns, corn-cribs, cabins—wherever four walls and a roof were found together." [69] Books were used for pillows. Carpets became saturated with blood from the dozens of men who lay shoulder to shoulder on them.

Female volunteers like Clara Barton and Mary Ann Bickerdyke aided army doctors and local medical men who cared for the injured. Medical procedures were crude and unsanitary, since no one yet understood the importance of sanitation, particularly sterile medical equipment. Injured men were usually carried, groaning in pain, to the surgeon, who examined their wounds with dirty hands and often opted for amputation as the quickest means of treatment. Many held bloody knives in their teeth and wiped them across their aprons between cases, tossing severed arms and legs to one side of the operating table until they could be buried. At the end of the operation, patients were usually laid on the ground to await transportation.

As a result, infection took a terrible toll; thousands died from complications from their wounds. "I believe the doctors kills more than they cure," one Alabama private said, "doctors h'ain't got half sense." [70]

Plight of the Wounded

Doctors performed heroically during the Civil War, but none were highly trained according to today's standards. A medical school course commonly lasted only two years, the second year often being a repeat of the first. Despite such limitations, William G. Stevenson, a Confederate surgeon, reveals intelligence and insight as he describes conditions at a Mississippi hospital in *In Hospital and Camp*, edited by Harold Elk Straubing.

During the week following the battle the wounded were brought in by hundreds, and the surgeons were overtasked. Above 5000 wounded men, demanding instant and constant attendance, made a call too great to be met successfully. A much larger proportion of amputations was performed than would have been necessary if the wounds could have received earlier attention. On account of exposure, many wounds were gangrenous when the patients reached the hospital. In these cases delay was fatal, and an operation almost equally so, as tetanus often followed speedily. Where amputation was performed, eight out of ten died. The deaths in Corinth averaged fifty per day for a week after the battle. While the surgeons, as a body, did their duty nobly, there were some young men, apparently just out of college, who performed difficult operations with the assurance and assumed skill of practiced surgeons, and with little regard for life or limb. In a few days erysipelas [a skin disease] broke out, and numbers died of it. Pneumonia, typhoid fever and measles followed. . . . As soon as possible, the wounded who could be moved were sent off to Columbus . . . and elsewhere, and some relief was thus obtained. We were also comforted by the arrival of a corps of nurses. Their presence acted like a charm. Order emerged from chaos, and in a few hours all looked cleaner and really felt better, from the skill and industry of a few devoted women.

"Forever Free"

Many people saw the Battle of Antietam as a stalemate rather than a Union victory, since both armies sustained huge losses and survived. Abraham Lincoln, who had hoped for a decisive Union victory, was enormously dissatisfied with the outcome, particularly after he learned that McClellan had held almost twenty thousand men in reserve throughout the fighting, never bringing them onto the field at all. Two months later, Lincoln lost patience with the young general's overcautiousness and permanently removed him from command. Little Mac would never lead an army again.

Despite his disappointment, Lincoln formally recognized the battle as a Union

Lincoln meets with McClellan at Antietam. Lincoln was greatly dissapointed in the general and removed him from command two months after the battle.

victory for the sake of a more important agenda—emancipation. The president had never been an abolitionist, but he despised slavery and realized that freeing slaves would be the morally right thing to do. Practically, emancipation would seriously damage the Southern economy and help bring the war to an end. It would also end the threat of European support for the Confederacy, since Britain and France (who had outlawed slavery in 1833 and 1848, respectively) would favor a nation that opposed slavery over one that defended it.

Convinced that the time was right, Lincoln issued the Emancipation Proclamation five days after the battle. "On the first day of January, in the year of our Lord one thousand eight hundred and sixty three, all persons held as slaves within any State or designated part of a State the people whereof shall then be in rebellion against the United States, shall be then, thenceforward, and forever free."[71]

Not surprisingly, the proclamation came under criticism. Slave owners proclaimed it detestable. Abolitionists complained that it did not go far enough, since it only applied to slaves in Confederate states.

Overall, however, the announcement had the effect for which Lincoln had hoped. European support for the Confederacy weakened. Northerners were exhilarated at the stand their government had taken. Blacks showed their gratitude

Proven to Be Men

During the Civil War, almost 180,000 black troops fought for the Union in 449 separate engagements. When the war was over, sixteen soldiers and four black sailors were awarded the newly instituted Medal of Honor for distinguished service. Despite their devotion to their country, however, most were constantly having to prove themselves, as author Noah Andre Trudeau explains in *Like Men of War.*

> Black units were used primarily for garrison duty because of the preconceived notions of most white officers. And when they *were* at last committed to action, they too often entered the fight saddled with the burden of having to prove themselves worthy to their Caucasian comrades. . . . From Port Hudson and Milliken's Bend in 1863 through Fort Blakely in 1865, black troops were ever having to prove anew that they would fight. . . .
>
> Given the opportunity, and with good leadership, black regiments did well in combat. In some cases, such as at Port Hudson and New Market Heights, they were deliberately committed to a hopeless task—not for any strategic reason, but solely to test their mettle. While it would be difficult to identify a major engagement in which black soldiers played a crucial role, it is clear that their courage and discipline saved [General Tru-

> man] Seymour's army from destruction at Olustee [Florida], their steadfastness made possible the Union victory at Fort Fisher, and their combativeness greatly contributed to the Federal capture of Fort Blakely. The best summary of this record of performance came from a trooper in the 5th Regiment Massachusetts Cavalry (Colored), who said, "The colored soldiers in this four years' struggle have proven themselves in every respect to be men."

Black soldiers were usually assigned garrison duty (pictured). When given the chance, however, they proved their courage and dignity in combat.

by enlisting to fight for the Union. By the end of the war, almost one hundred eighty thousand had served in both the army and the navy.

"Will the slave fight? If any man asks you, tell him No. But if anyone asks you will a Negro fight, tell him Yes,"[72] one individual proudly declared. And another said, "This year has brought about many changes that at the beginning would have been thought impossible. The close of the year finds me a soldier for the cause of my race. May God bless the cause, and enable me in the coming year to forward it on."[73]

Chapter 4

Battle of Gettysburg

y the summer of 1863, Robert E. Lee thought of his Army of Northern Virginia as a virtually unconquerable force. It had survived McClellan and his much vaunted Peninsula Campaign and had defeated the Army of the Potomac at Manassas, Fredericksburg, and Chancellorsville. It had overcome the enemy's superior numbers by finding his weak spots and hitting him hard.

The Union army, on the other hand, had been demoralized by constant defeats and by commanders who hesitated to fight and take risks. George McClellan had been intimidated by what he believed to be the South's superior numbers. Ambrose Burnside lacked the self-confidence and ability to lead a mighty army. Major General Joseph E. Hooker, the most recent to command the Army of the Potomac, lost his nerve during the Battle of Chancellorsville and allowed Lee's fewer than sixty thousand men to soundly defeat his larger force.

"All-or-Nothing Thrust"

Despite the South's victories, however, Lee knew that the Confederacy remained the underdog in the war. After two years, his home state of Virginia lay in waste, its citizens exhausted and its farms depleted. Out west, Ulysses S. Grant had laid siege to Confederate-held Vicksburg, Mississippi. Its capture would mean Union control of the Mississippi River and a split of the South. The North, although tired of the conflict, had plenty of men and matériel for its armies and could fight on indefinitely if the war continued.

To even the odds, Lee devised a daring plan. He would march north into Pennsylvania, where he would threaten Philadelphia and Baltimore, cut communications between Washington and the rest of the country, and force Hooker and his army to attack. In doing so, he hoped to draw the fighting away from Virginia, giving it relief from the war for a time. He also hoped to pull Union troops away from Grant's offensive at Vicksburg; perhaps scare Northern politicians into suing for peace.

Lee understood the risk he was taking. If successful, the offensive could bring about Southern victory. If his army was captured, the Confederacy would inevitably fall. Still, he believed the time was right to throw the North off balance by doing something unexpected, and invading the North smacked of power and invincibility. Bruce Catton writes, "[It would be] an all-or-nothing thrust simply because both friend and foe were bound to look at it that way. . . . When [Lee's army] went north they carried the undeveloped climax of the war with them. Win or lose, this march was going to take them to the high-water mark." [74]

The Opponents

Much of Lee's confidence was based on his subordinate generals, who were seasoned veterans—solid, dependable James Longstreet, whom Lee called "my old warhorse"; [75] A. P. Hill, who always wore a red shirt into battle; Richard Ewell, a fiery little man with one leg who had himself strapped to his horse going into battle; and flamboyant cavalry leader Jeb Stuart, who served as Lee's scout when the army was on the move.

Stuart, "the eyes and ears of my army," [76] according to Lee, proved a hindrance to the Confederate leader this time. A charming, gallant, and courageous soldier, easily recognizable by his yellow sash, beplumed hat, and huge mustache complete with upcurled tips, Stuart saw the war as an exciting adventure. "We must substitute *esprit* [enthusiasm] for numbers," he explained, "Therefore, I strive to inculcate [instill] in my men the spirit of the chase." [77]

Early in 1862, he and his cavalry had managed an audacious three-day, one-hundred-fifty-mile sweep around McClellan's huge army, capturing horses and wagons, cutting

The industrialized North was better able to supply weaponry to its troops than was the South, as this well-stocked Union arsenal shows.

telegraph wires, and symbolically thumbing their noses at the enemy. As the Army of Northern Virginia marched into Pennsylvania in the last weeks of June, Stuart decided to repeat his performance, circling the army where it reportedly lay in camp in Maryland, then catching up to Lee in a few days. Stuart's excursion took him and his men far from the main party, however, and unexpected delays kept him from informing Lee that the Army of the Potomac was hot on the Confederates' heels. Lee, who assumed that Stuart would notify him of any real threat, relaxed and directed his army to spread out and let its presence be felt in the Pennsylvania countryside.

Not only was the Federal army on the march, it was no longer led by Joseph Hooker, whom Lee had faced two months previously. The Union army's defeat at Chancellorsville had unnerved "Fighting Joe," and Lincoln had replaced him with General George Gordon Meade, who was reputedly a fearless fighter. Forty-eight-year-old Meade, known to his men as that "damned old goggle-eyed snapping turtle," [78]

had a quick temper and a sharp tongue, he constantly alienated his men, and he had never commanded an army the size of the Army of the Potomac before. Nevertheless, Lincoln believed that he was the best choice to bring about Lee's destruction.

Meade had under his command Generals John F. Reynolds, Winfield Scott Hancock, Daniel F. Sickles, George Sykes, John Sedgwick, Oliver O. Howard, and Henry W. Slocum, some of whom had served beside him under Hooker, but none of whom felt the personal loyalty to him as Lee's men did to their leader.

The First Day

The opening shots of the battle of Gettysburg were fired on July 1, 1863, when both Lee and Meade were more than a dozen miles away from the little market town located at a crossroads in the Pennsylvania countryside. Confederate advance guards—

A view of the small town of Gettysburg, taken from Cemetery Hill after the battle. The tents on the right are hospital shelters, where the wounded were treated.

part of A. P. Hill's corps—came in from the north that morning, hoping to find shoes to replace some of their badly worn footwear. They were unaware that elements of General John Buford's Union cavalry already occupied Gettysburg. The two sides met and clashed on the town's outskirts, throwing residents into a panic. "People were running here and there screaming that the town would be shelled," a Gettysburg woman recalled. "No one knew where to go or what to do. My husband went to the garden and picked a mess of beans . . . for he declared the Rebels should not have *one*." [79]

While skirmishing continued, couriers from both sides hurried off for reinforcements. When Lee received word that the Federals were within striking distance, he rode to the scene of the fight with no real intention of continuing the attack. Half of his own army was still on the road, and, since Jeb Stuart and his cavalry scouts were not present to give him much-needed information, Lee had no idea exactly where Meade and the rest of the Federals lay. Nevertheless, Hill's men appeared to be pushing the enemy back, so Lee seized the moment and ordered an all-out offensive. In an enthusiastic push,

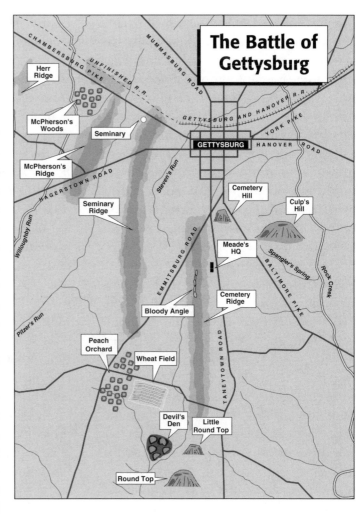

The Battle of Gettysburg

his troops drove the Federals into the hills to the south, where the bluecoats threw up defenses and waited for another attack that they were convinced would inevitably come before nightfall.

It did not, however. Always polite, Lee had suggested rather than commanded Richard Ewell, who had taken part in that morning's assault, to head up an attack that afternoon if he felt it were practical.

Ewell considered. What was left of his leg was infected and causing him pain. His men had suffered heavy losses and were tired after hours of fighting. Some of his backup troops had not yet arrived. Thus, he chose to ignore Lee's suggestion, and as night fell, the two great armies slowly gathered and took up positions—Lee's sixty-five-thousand-man force to the north and east of town; Meade's eighty-five thousand Federals entrenched on Culp's Hill and Cemetery Hill, due south of Gettysburg.

Meade himself arrived at Cemetery Hill shortly after midnight. After a quick reconnaissance, he decided that the Union position was a good one. His men held the high ground, including Cemetery Ridge, a rise that ran southward and ended at the summit of two rocky, scrub-covered hills known as Round Top and Little Round Top. In these positions, the Federals were above their enemy, better able to fend off coming assaults than if they were in a more vulnerable position below. Gettysburg itself was occupied by Confederates, but Meade did not really care who possessed the town. It was the next day's battle that occupied his mind that night.

The Second Day

Lee was confident on July 2 as he and his staff prepared for the second day of battle. The previous day's struggle had been a Southern triumph; the Virginian hoped that this day's fight would prove as suc-

cessful. He favored a frontal assault, despite General Longstreet's having advised him to send a portion of his men around the Union flank (side) to strike Meade from the rear. Lee disagreed. Jeb Stuart had not yet arrived, so no one knew the strength of Meade's forces or exactly where he had stationed them. Lee opted to strike the Union force on its flanks, where it might be weaker, but he would do it head on.

With that decided, Lee ordered an early attack. Ewell and Longstreet, however, took some time getting their forces into position, and it was afternoon before they struck. Ewell led his men up Culp's Hill while Longstreet attacked Union general Sickles, whom Meade had ordered to hold Little Round Top, but who had chosen to take up a position on a rise a half mile ahead of the rest of the army. In this precarious position, the Federals were hit from three sides. The men fought valiantly, struggling in the Peach Orchard, Devil's Den (a hazardous-looking tumble of boulders), and the Valley of Death. Sickles's only salvation was a battalion of Minnesotans who gave their lives to hold the Confederates back. "The balls were whizzing so thick that it looked like a man could hold out a hat and catch it full," remembered one Texan. Another soldier recalled, "The hoarse and indistinguishable orders of commanding officers, the screaming and bursting of shells . . . the death screams of wounded animals, the groans of their human companions, . . . a perfect hell on earth, never, perhaps to be equaled . . . not *ever* to be forgotten in a man's lifetime."[80]

Meanwhile, the rest of Longstreet's Confederates were determined to take the all-but-undefended Little Round Top. From its heights they could shell the Federals on Cemetery Ridge and perhaps chalk up another day's victory. Sent in to reconnoiter for the Federals, General G. K. Warren saw the grayclads moving up the slope of the hill and dashed off for reinforcements. He was able to commandeer four regiments, among them the 20th Maine, led by scholarly colonel Joshua Lawrence Chamberlain. Chamberlain and

fewer than four hundred men were ordered to hold Little Round Top at all costs, and, in the next two hours, he and his outnumbered troops faced some of the fiercest fighting of the war. Forty thousand rounds of ammunition were fired on the slope of the hill in less than an hour and a half. One third of Chamberlain's men were killed. He remembered, "The edge of the conflict swayed to and fro with wild whirlpools and eddies. At times I saw around me more of the enemy than of my own men; gaps opening, swallowing, closing again; squads of stalwart men who had cut their way through us, disappearing as if translated. All around, a strange, mingled roar."[81]

In the end, Little Round Top was saved after Chamberlain resorted to an almost forgotten textbook offensive in which his men plunged wildly down the mountainside,

Confederate soldiers (right) advance on Little Round Top. From its heights, Southern cannon would be able to bombard Northern troops on Cemetery Ridge.

swept back the Confederates, and secured the promontory for the Union.

Devil's Den, the Valley of Death, and Little Round Top were not the only sites of savage fighting that day. In the evening, on the crest of Cemetery Ridge, A. P. Hill's men managed to seize heavy artillery from Federals, only to be beaten back after Meade sent in reinforcements to recapture the positions. On the Union's right flank, the Federals fought all day to hold Culp's Hill, but by nightfall Ewell and his Confederates had gained a toehold halfway up the rise and were preparing to attack again the next morning.

Interim

That night, the moon shone dimly through the smoke that lingered from the day's fighting, and the countryside rang with the cries of wounded and dying men. Meade and Lee met with staff in their respective camps to assess progress and formulate plans for the following morning.

Meade was cautiously optimistic and determined to go on fighting. Union losses had been great, but Confederate losses were greater. Lee's men had not been able to break even the weakest points of the Federal line and had not repeated their victory of the day before. The irascible general saw no reason that his bluecoats could not go on the offensive the next morning if Lee did not attack first.

Lee knew that if he failed to continue fighting, he would be admitting defeat. The situation was not to his liking —he had

not been able to choose his locale, prepare elaborate defenses, and strike at the enemy's weak spots as he usually did—but he was convinced that the Union army's morale was low after two days of profitless bloodshed. He also assumed that Meade, like Union generals before him, would retreat if given one more hard push.

With that in mind, Lee decided to consolidate his army and smash at the center of Meade's lines, from which men had been taken to defend the Federal right and left flanks. Lee chose General George Pickett, a part of Longstreet's force, to lead the attack. At the same time, Ewell and his men would continue their push up Culp's Hill, while Jeb Stuart and his cavalrymen, who had finally arrived, would dash around the Union right and strike from behind.

Not everyone supported the audacious plan. Longstreet in particular told Lee that a frontal attack at the Union's strongest point would be suicidal. "Old Peter," as he was affectionately called, was reliable and a hard fighter, but he could be stubborn as well. Desperately, he tried to convince Lee of his error. "I have been a soldier all my life. I have been with soldiers engaged in fights by couples, by squads, companies, regiments, divisions, and armies, and should know as well as anyone what soldiers can do. It is my opinion that no 15,000 men ever arrayed for battle can take that position."[82] Pickett, who was to lead the charge, kept his thoughts to himself, but scribbled a note to his fiancée just prior to going into bat-tle. "If Old Peter's nod means death, then good-bye and God bless you, little one."[83]

Lee, however, was convinced his plan would work. He believed that his men could accomplish anything he asked them to do. It was an assumption he bit-terly regretted before the next day was over.

The Third Day

Again, all did not go according to plan on July 3. Lee had counted on Ewell's assault on Culp's Hill to coordinate with Pickett's and Stuart's offensives, but it took several hours to get Pickett's men and other sup-porting troops into position. Ewell, who was face to face with the enemy on the slope of the hill, could not wait. He and his men attacked at first light (about 4:00 A.M.), fought fiercely for seven hours, then retreated under a hail of deadly rifle fire long before the major attack on the Union center even began.

As noon approached, a heavy silence fell over the valley. A few minutes after one o'clock, a white puff of smoke rose from a Confed-erate cannon, the signal that

the main Southern offensive was about to begin. One minute later, Lee's big guns, one hundred forty strong, opened fire si-multaneously along a two-mile line. Bruce Catton writes, "Every gun in the Confeder-ate line went off, in one long rolling crash—the loudest noise, probably, that had ever been heard on the North Ameri-can continent up to that moment. The most stupendous bombardment of the Civil War had begun."[84]

The barrage was intended to terrify and confuse the Federals, but they were prepared and quickly set off their own heavy artillery. The two-hour-long can-nonade left the entire valley full of smoke, which eddied and swirled long af-ter the big guns were silent again. When the smoke lifted, the Federals steadied their rifles and took aim. Thirteen thou-sand Confederates marched silently across the fields and up Cemetery Ridge

As Union troops lie protected behind a stone wall on Cemetery Ridge, Confederate soldiers led by General George Pickett begin their charge.

in the great assault that would be remembered as Pickett's Charge. A Union officer described their approach:

> More than half a mile their front extends . . . man touching man, rank pressing rank. . . . The red flags wave, the horsemen gallop up and down, . . . the arms of (thirteen) thousand men, barrel and bayonet, gleam in the sun, a sloping forest of flashing steel. Right on they move . . . over ridge and slope, through orchard and meadow, and cornfield, magnificent, grim, irresistible.[85]

A small clump of trees stood right in the center of the Union lines, and it was toward those trees that the Confederates headed. They moved at a brisk, steady pace, in the words of one survivor, as if "we had nothing to do but march unopposed to Cemetery (Hill) and occupy it."[86]

Union infantrymen were waiting for them behind the solid protection of a stone wall. Gunners, poised over their cannon, held their fire until the advancing line was perilously close and then touched match to fuse. Shells flew, and a mighty groan went up from the field as hundreds of men were hit in the first instant of the battle. As many as ten men at a time were killed by a single shell exploding in their midst. "We could not help hitting them at every shot,"[87] one officer recalled.

Pickett's men never had a chance, but they put up a terrific fight. "Men fire into each other's faces not five feet apart," a survivor wrote of the fighting. "There are bayonet thrusts, sabre strokes, pistol shots . . . men going down on their hands and knees, spinning round like tops, throwing out their arms, gulping blood, falling; legless, armless, headless. There are ghastly heaps of dead men."[88]

It was a murderous engagement. Smoke from thousands of guns billowed and boiled, cutting off visibility except at close quarters. Muskets, knapsacks, and fragments of human bodies flew through the air. One group of three hundred, led by General Lewis Armistead, managed to break through the Union lines near the clump of trees, but the push was short lived. Most of the men were cut down or taken prisoner, and Armistead himself was killed.

Confederate dead litter the field after Gettysburg. Pickett never forgave Lee for the loss of his division during the charge up Cemetery Ridge.

Repelled by strong Union defenses, those Confederates who survived the assault staggered back to safety, leaving their wounded on the field. They were met by Lee, who had watched the fiasco and was quick to accept blame. "It was all my fault,"[89] he said, and later offered his resignation to Jefferson Davis, explaining that a younger man could perhaps do a better job. Davis rejected the offer.

By evening when the battle ended, half of the thirteen thousand Confederates who made Pickett's charge had been wounded, killed, or captured. In some companies, not a single man returned unhurt. When Lee told Pickett to gather his division for a possible counterattack that evening, Pickett replied, "General Lee, I *have* no division now," and never forgave the general for what had happened to his men that day. "That old man had my division slaughtered at Gettysburg,"[90] he remarked years later.

Indisputably, victory lay with the Union that day. The Confederates were beaten. They had lost one-third of their numbers and would have been hard pressed to fight again the next day, although Lee gamely prepared for such an attack.

Meade had no intention of engaging the enemy a fourth time, however. Lacking the insight to see that the total destruction of Lee's army was necessary to end the war, he was happy simply to have won the battle. Thus he allowed the Army of Northern Virginia to retreat. After the

For the Good of His Country

On August 8, 1863, after successfully getting his battered army back to the safety of Virginia, Robert E. Lee offered to resign as head of the Army of Northern Virginia, citing his failure at the Battle of Gettysburg. President Jefferson Davis rejected the offer. Lee's letter to the Confederate president is included in *The Wartime Papers of R. E. Lee*, edited by Clifford Dowdey.

The general remedy for the want of success in a military commander is his removal. This is natural, and in many instances proper. For no matter what may be the ability of the officer, if he loses the confidence of his troops disaster must sooner or later follow.

I have been prompted by these reflections more than once since my return from Pennsylvania to propose to Your Excellency the propriety of selecting another commander for this army. I have seen and heard of expressions of discontent in the public journals at the result of the expedition. I do not know how far this feeling extends in the army. My brother officers have been too kind to report it, and so far the troops have been too generous to exhibit it. It is fair, however, to suppose that it does exist, and success is so necessary to us that nothing should be risked to secure it. I therefore, in all sincerity, request Your Excellency to take measures to supply my place. . . .

I have no complaints to make of any one but myself. I have received nothing but kindness from those above me, and the most considerate attention from my comrades and companions in arms. To Your Excellency I am specially indebted for uniform kindness and consideration. . . .

I am very respectfully and truly yours,

R.E. Lee
General

Confederates had slipped to safety across the Potomac, he declared himself satisfied to have driven the enemy off "home soil." On hearing the news, Lincoln remarked angrily to his private secretary, John Hay: "Will our generals never get the idea out of their heads? The whole country is our soil."[91]

"Canned Hellfire"

Gettysburg was, according to some historians, the most monumental battle ever fought on North American soil. It lasted three days and involved 150,000 men. Those Federals killed, wounded, or missing totaled twenty-three thousand; Confederate casualties equaled more than twenty thousand, and both armies came out of the battle significantly weakened. The Union lost thousands of seasoned fighting men and had to rely on inexperienced and unwilling draftees for months to come. The thousands that Lee sacrificed were irreplaceable, since the South had no way of replenishing its numbers.

The enormity of the loss was in a large part due to the weapons used in the conflict. Technology in this field reached new heights in the Civil War, and fighting men faced a terrifying array of guns, bullets, shells, and missiles when they went into battle. For targets up to a mile away, heavy artillery such as cannon and mortars hurled solid iron balls (solid shot) or blasted exploding shells that scattered red-hot fragments. Exploding shells usually burst in the air and included shrapnel, a thin-walled shell filled with iron balls, and canister, sheet-metal tubes filled with hundreds of lead slugs. Canister was most effective for close-range targets. Under such deadly fire, even soldiers who threw themselves to the ground were likely to get hit by falling chunks of metal, which some called "canned hellfire."[92]

Heavy artillery was a vital part of almost every battle, but the newly invented Gatling

Heavy artillery such as this cannon was responsible for much of the loss of life on both sides.

gun, named for its creator Richard Gatling, could also be a deadly addition to an army's arsenal. The Gatling gun was essentially six to ten rifle barrels mounted around a single shaft with ammunition fed into the chambers from a long cartridge belt called a magazine. When cranked rapidly, the gun could spit out up to six hundred rounds per minute, becoming a rapid-fire weapon that could kill hundreds of men in the time it took to load and fire an ordinary rifle. Even with such advantages, however, the Gatling gun was used for only a short time during the war. Bruce Catton explains, "The officers in charge of the Ordnance Department in the United States were pretty conservative. They didn't believe in a gun like this. It was bound to break down. So they did not put any reliance in it and it dropped out of use, to be revived again only after the war."[93]

Despite the importance of heavy artillery, handheld weapons were an essential part of a soldier's gear, although Confederates sometimes lacked the ammunition needed to fire theirs. Especially in the North, old smooth bore muskets were replaced with modern rifles, so called because of the rifling—spiral grooves—cut inside the barrel. Such grooves caused bullets to spin in flight, and gave the soldiers greater range and accuracy when they fired. Breech-loading rifles, in which bullets are inserted near the trigger rather than the mouth of the gun, were increasingly popular among Northern soldiers, as were repeating ri-

fles (rifles that fired several bullets without reloading). Bullets improved, too, with Minie balls—inch-long, soft-lead bullets with pointed tips and hollow bases—replacing the round lead balls that had been used in earlier wars.

Such advances in weaponry gave a heavy advantage to the defending army, since entrenched men could now fire at and hit the enemy before he got too close. Bayonets, which had been vital in earlier wars, were now less frequently used, since they required hand-to-hand combat. Many generals were slow to grasp the idea that battles could effectively be fought from a distance with such new weaponry, and they continued to order their men to charge the enemy. The results were the tragically high losses such as those recorded at Gettysburg.

Burying the Dead

The task of caring for those who were wounded at Gettysburg was a colossal one, but managing the dead posed an equally difficult problem. In the days after the battle, overworked burial parties labored to inter thousands of decaying bodies in shallow trenches, but friends and relatives, looking for lost loved ones, undermined the work by uncovering the graves. Thus, mangled, bloated corpses lay scattered helter-skelter; grave robbers picked over the remains; and the smell of death and putrefaction blanketed the region.

Pennsylvania governor Andrew G. Curtin visited the area a week after the battle and was horrified by sights and smells he encountered. In an attempt to establish order and decorum, he quickly approved a plan to purchase land to be used as a cemetery for those who died in battle. Contractors were hired to place the bodies in coffins, then rebury them in neat concentric arcs with headstones lying flush with the ground. (Some bodies were claimed by relatives or shipped to soldiers' hometowns.) The work proceeded slowly—no more than one hundred bodies were buried each day—so that by the time Lincoln dedicated the ground in mid-November, only a third of the new cemetery was finished. The work was finally completed on March 18, 1864, and records show that more than thirty-five hundred Civil War dead, many with their names unknown, lay buried on the site of what was once a bloody battlefield.

"The Last Full Measure of Devotion"

Gettysburg proved to be the climax of the Civil War. The Union with its enormous reserves of men and matériel, and with seasoned generals who were willing to fight, had begun to dispel the myth of Southern invincibility. Southern morale, though still high, was shaken. The Confederacy's growing destitution and lack of manpower prevented Lee from ever again mounting a major offensive against the North.

The Confederate general paid a heavy price for the miscalculations he made in going to war against the North in the summer of 1863. He had believed that his men could win, and had lost a third of his force as a result. Not only had he misjudged the North's strength, he had had to suffer the news of Grant's capture of Vicksburg on the same day his defeated men began their retreat to Virginia. He had underestimated Lincoln's commitment to restoring the Union, and he now realized that the president, rather than suing for peace, would fight to the death for the sake of reinstating national unity.

Lincoln reiterated his commitment to restoring the Union in a few appropriate remarks, delivered on November 19, 1863, to a crowd of six thousand who had gathered at the Gettysburg battlefield to commemorate the new Union cemetery there. The message lasted only two minutes, but Lincoln's simple yet elegant words stirred the deepest feelings of Americans everywhere.

It is for us the living . . . to be dedicated here to the unfinished work which they who fought here have thus far so nobly advanced. It is rather for us to be here dedicated to the great task remaining before us—that from these honored dead we take increased devotion to that cause for which they gave the last full measure of devotion.[94]

Chapter 5

Siege of Vicksburg

onths before George Meade and Robert E. Lee met on the battlefield at Gettysburg, Abraham Lincoln pointed to a map illustrating the western theater of the war—territory west of the Appalachian Mountains—and observed, "See what a lot of land these fellows [the Confederates] hold, of which Vicksburg is the key. . . . Let us get Vicksburg and all that country is ours. The war can never be brought to a close until that key is in our pocket."[95]

The key of which he spoke—Vicksburg, Mississippi—was a rather ordinary town of some five thousand people, set on high bluffs above the east bank of the Mississippi River, just where it made a hairpin turn, almost doubling back on itself. The town had its share of cotton warehouses, banks, hotels, shops, and businesses, many of them related to river traffic. The courthouse, a

convent, and two churches were perched atop the hills. Honeysuckle-wreathed homes of the well-to-do sat aloof from poorer neighborhoods that lay along the water's edge. Sternwheeler riverboats regularly moored along the docks.

Abraham Lincoln called the city of Vicksburg (pictured) the key to winning the war.

Vicksburg was unique, however, because it was a link that connected the eastern and western parts of the Confederacy and because it sat on a major transportation route—the Mississippi River. By October 1862, the Union had gained control of the lower parts of the Mississippi, but Confederates held a stretch of more than a hundred miles between Port Hudson and Vicksburg. They thus prevented normal traffic up and down the river and effectively cut the flow of Northern goods to and from New Orleans.

Not only was Vicksburg strategically placed, it was also a fortress. The town boasted forty newly installed cannon, pointing riverward, to threaten any Union gunboats that might try to attack from that direction. On the landward side, forts, trenches, and other defenses had been constructed to stave off an attack from the east. Land to the north was swampy and full of poisonous snakes and mosquitoes that carried malaria and yellow fever, impediments to even the strongest army.

U. S. Grant

Union general Ulysses S. Grant, head of the Department of the Tennessee, agreed with Lincoln that Vicksburg had to be taken. Grant was a quiet, unremarkable Midwesterner who loved horses, disliked uniforms, and was devoted to his wife, Julia, who was at his side at every possible opportunity during the war. He had been a virtual failure before 1861—a military

Vicksburg was defended by forty cannon such as this one.

man who drank too much when he was bored, a farmer who could not harvest enough from his land to support his family, an earnest but unenterprising clerk who was working in his father's harness shop in Galena, Illinois, when the South seceded.

With the coming of war, however, Grant found his calling. He earned the nickname "Unconditional Surrender" for his resoluteness in dealing with the enemy during the capture of Fort Donelson, Tennessee, in February 1862, then was promoted to head of the Army of the Tennessee in October 1862 after his triumph at the Battle of Shiloh (Pittsburg Landing, Tennessee) in April. "I can't spare this man, he *fights*," [96] Lincoln responded when newspapers called for his removal after the bloody battle.

While Grant lacked the charisma that made leaders like George McClellan and Robert E. Lee beloved by their men, he was admired and respected by his troops, who knew that he was single-minded in his objective—complete, uncompromising victory over the enemy. "His soldiers do not salute him, they only watch him, with a certain sort of familiar reverence. [They] observe him coming and, rising to their feet, gather on each side of the way to see him pass," [97] one reporter wrote.

A Determined Leader

Grant's initial plan to take Vicksburg was straightforward—divide his army into two parts and attack from the north. His friend and trusted subordinate, William Tecumseh Sherman, would head one column while Grant himself led the other. The plan fell apart when put into practice, however. Pushing due south, Grant's supply lines were cut by the Confederates, forcing his retreat back to Memphis. Sherman's men were defeated by a superior force at Chickasaw Bluffs, north of Vicksburg.

With characteristic tenacity, Grant did not give up. He tried to get his forty-five-thousand-man army to Vicksburg four times over a period of several months, but got no farther than Young's Point, twenty miles north of the town on the wrong side of the river. Union engineers even attempted to dig a canal across the hairpin bend that would allow acting Rear Admiral David D. Porter's navy ships, stranded in the Mississippi north of Vicksburg, to bypass the town and attack from the south. The strenuous effort of digging the mile-long ditch kept Grant's men in peak condition throughout the winter, but the project proved impractical and never worked.

As spring arrived, Grant's determination hardened, and he requested that Porter make an all-out effort to get his navy fleet downriver. While Porter readied his ships, Grant himself marched his men south through Louisiana. Below Vicksburg, the navy would ferry his men across the river, after which they would march north and come in on Vicksburg from the east.

It was a complex plan, and it worked. Porter's fleet, moving at top speed under cover of darkness, survived an all-out Confederate barrage that threatened to sink them, met up with Grant south of Vicksburg on April 30, 1863, and got the Federals across the Mississippi. "When (the crossing) was effected, I felt a degree of relief scarcely ever equaled since . . . ," Grant admitted. "I was now in the enemy's country, with a river and the stronghold of Vicksburg between me and my base of supplies. But I was on dry ground on the same side of the river with the enemy."[98]

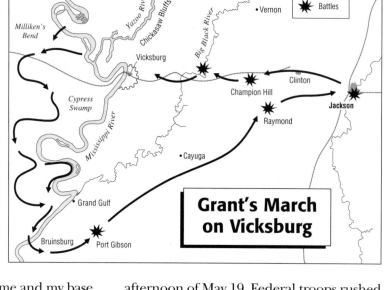

Grant's March on Vicksburg

Assault on a Fortress

With the first step of his offensive behind him, Grant severed communication with the North and marched his army in an almost two-hundred-mile loop through Mississippi, cutting rail and communication lines and scattering Confederate forces, all in an effort to prevent reinforcement of Vicksburg. In three weeks he fought and won five battles—at Port Gibson, Raymond, Jackson (the state capital), Champion Hill, and Big Black River. On May 18, his forces had looped back within striking distance of Vicksburg, and Grant ordered a direct assault by Sherman's corps, who was positioned northeast of the town. In mid-

afternoon of May 19, Federal troops rushed the town's defenses but were hampered by hundreds of fallen trees, purposefully cut by Confederates. Some Federals got close enough to plant a United States flag near a Confederate fort that guarded the road, but heavy fire from Vicksburg's defenders soon pushed them back again. By evening, Federal casualties totaled nearly one thousand, and Sherman drew back to reassess the situation.

Three days later, Grant attempted a second assault on the town. First came a four-hour bombardment by heavy artillery, then Union infantry attacked along a three-mile front. Again Vicksburg's defenses proved impenetrable. This time Union losses numbered more than three thousand, and Grant realized that further attempts to storm the town would prove equally unproductive. In a change of tactics, he resolved to outwait the enemy, and to that aim he directed his men to block all possible routes into and out of town.

The Siege

Grant's decision to besiege Vicksburg had nothing to do with sitting passively, waiting for its leaders to surrender. He hated boredom, and he knew that his troops could be better used fighting battles in other theaters of the war. To speed the fall of the town, he thus directed his forces to bombard it constantly from both the river and landward sides. One resident described the shelling:

To speed Vicksburg's fall, Grant ordered his artillery to bombard the town from gunboats on the river as well as from land-based cannon.

Bombshells in the form of huge iron spheres weighing nearly three hundred pounds and filled with gunpowder flew through the air, their burning fuses leaving a trail of smoke by day and of fire by night. A peculiar hissing, screaming noise accompanied their flight and, exploding with tremendous violence, they wrecked houses and streets "like small earthquakes."[99]

A Confederate soldier inside the town wrote, "The place was a perfect pandemonium from early dawn. The hoarse bellowing of the mortars, the sharp report of rifled artillery, the scream and explosion of every variety of deadly missiles, intermingled with the incessant, sharp reports of small-arms."[100]

The physical damage to Vicksburg caused by such constant shelling was stupendous. Homes and businesses were destroyed, and by the end of the barrage, few buildings remained that had not been struck by a shell at least once. Trees were blasted. Streets, yards, and gardens turned into stretches of wasteland. Women, children, and slaves huddled together, tended each other's wounds, and tried to survive. One woman wrote in her journal:

A horrible day. We were all in the cellar when a shell came tearing through the roof, burst up-stairs, tore up that room and the pieces coming through both floors down into the cellar, tore open the leg of (my husband's pants). On the heels of this came Mr. J. to tell us that young Mrs. P. had her thighbone crushed. When Martha went for the milk, she came back horror-stricken to tell us that the black girl had her arm taken off by a shell.[101]

Cave Dwellers

To avoid being killed, residents dug caves into the yellow clay of the town's hillsides; at one count more than five hundred such hideouts existed. One resident observed that

Caves were the fashion—the rage—over besieged Vicksburg. Negroes . . . hired themselves out to dig them, at from thirty to fifty dollars, according to size. Many persons . . . would sell them [the caves] to others, who had been less fortunate . . . and so great was the demand for cave workmen, that a new branch of industry sprang up and became popular.[102]

Some caves were simple holes where women and children cowered at night or when the shelling targeted their neighborhoods. Others were more permanent dwellings, consisting of several rooms furnished with rugs, chairs, and beds and staffed by family slaves.

Caves possessed their own particular dangers, however. "We were in hourly dread of snakes," one cave dweller wrote. "A large rattlesnake was found one morning under a mattress on which some of us had slept all night."[103] Cave dwellers also lived with the threat of collapse. Their dens were usually five to eight feet below the surface of the ground, but a direct hit from a shell could send the dirt ceiling crashing down, burying anyone caught inside.

Since supplies had been cut off by Grant's blockade, food soon ran low among the town's residents, but they bravely made do with what they could find. In the beginning, meager rations of meat, milk, vegetables, and flour were available, but as time passed and reserves ran low, corn meal and rice became staples. One woman wrote, "[I am] so tired of corn bread, which I never liked, that I eat it with tears in my eyes."[104] By the end

The Pride of Our Hearts

Caves were the shelters of choice during the siege of Vicksburg. Some were mere holes in the ground, others were moderately large. One of the most elaborate, described by its owner as "the pride of our hearts," is described in A. A. Hoehling's *Vicksburg: 47 Days of Siege.*

There was, first, an open walk, with parapet six feet high cut into the hillside. In one wall of this was a low and narrow opening overhung by creeping vines and shaded by papaw-trees. This was our side door. Here the rector smoked his coconut pipe, and the children made mud-pies and played with paper dolls cut from a few picture-papers and magazines that happened somehow to be among our belongings.

This cave ran about twenty feet underground, and communicated at right angles with a wing which opened on the front of the hill, giving us a free circulation of air. At the door was an arbor of branches, in which, on a pine table, we dined when the shelling permitted. Near it were a dug-out fireplace and an open-air kitchen, with table, pans, etc. In the wall of the cave were a small closet for provisions and some niches for candles, books, and flowers. We always kept in tin cups bunches of wild flowers, berries, or bright leaves which the children gather in their walks. Our cave was strongly boarded at the entrances, and we had procured some mattresses which made comfortable beds. For a time we slept in the tent, [however] and only used the cave for shelter.

A woman prays for deliverance from the bombardment, which has forced her and other residents of Vicksburg underground.

of the siege, many of the most desperate had taken to eating dogs and wild birds, and mule meat was considered a luxury.

The psychological effects of such a life eventually wore down even the strongest optimists. "We are utterly cut off from the world, surrounded by a circle of fire," one woman wrote. "The fiery shower of shells goes on, day and night. . . . People do nothing but eat what they can get, sleep *when* they can, and dodge the shells." Another woman, feeling the effects of living in a cave for weeks on end, wrote, "It was living like plant roots."[105]

Behind the Breastworks

In the Confederate trenches, life was equally as bad. Confederate general John C. Pemberton and his army of thirty thousand, the sole military defenders of the town, were badly in need of outside reinforcements, which had been promised but were slow in coming. In order to prevent an overrun of the town's defenses by Grant's larger force, every available man had been assigned the arduous task of remaining on duty and on guard. Author A. A. Hoehling writes:

> The troops were . . . compelled to remain behind the breastworks and in the rifle pits for weeks without removing from their crouching positions, and subject to the different changes of weather. Very often a storm would rise, and the rain come pouring down, drenching them to the skin, and they would be unable to leave the works for the purpose of changing their clothing, but were compelled to remain in their damp and unhealthy garments, until the sun shone again and dried them.[106]

Food soon ran short in the trenches, and men subsisted on mule meat and a crude kind of bread made of "cow peas," a type of bean used to feed animals. Many became weak and ill from poor nutrition, exposure to the elements, and a lack of exercise. Untold numbers of troops developed malaria, yellow fever, dysentery, and pneumonia.

The Enemy Within

The struggle against disease was a common problem for both Northern and Southern armies throughout the country, but Vicksburg, with its surrounding rivers and bayous, was a particularly unhealthy locale. Men were always getting sick for a variety of reasons. Many new recruits were country boys who had never been exposed to disease. Any resistance they developed was eventually worn down by poor nutrition and constant exposure to the elements. Southern troops were usually

Union soldiers line up at mealtime. During the siege of Vicksburg, Union troops had enough to eat, unlike their Confederate counterparts.

on the brink of starvation and lived on green corn or bacon and hard biscuits for months at a time. Northern soldiers usually had enough to eat (perhaps even a few luxuries after the arrival of a package from home) but relied on an unbalanced diet of salt pork, hardtack (a hard biscuit), and black coffee.

At all times, sleeping conditions were fairly uncomfortable. Tents and blankets did little to ward off winter rain and cold, and summer heat coupled with disease-carrying insects were a deadly combination in the South. Housed in camps where conditions were dirty and crowded, washing was an unheard-of luxury, and toilet-facilities were trenches open to flies and other pests, men succumbed to the many ailments that came along—typhoid fever, dysentery, colds, flu, pneumonia, and such childhood illnesses as measles and chicken pox.

Since medicine and medical treatment were usually in short supply, many cases proved unexpectedly fatal. Half of all deaths in the war—more than three hundred thousand—were caused by illness. Those who survived often lived in a chronic state of ill health, as one member of the Army of the Potomac testified. "One of the wonders of these times was the army cough. . . . (It) would break out . . . when the men awoke, and it is almost a literal fact that when one hundred thousand men began to stir at reveille, the sound of their coughing would drown that of the beating drums."[107]

Risky Pastimes

Throughout the month of June, Union guns fired unceasingly on Vicksburg, while Grant's men managed to slowly inch closer to the Confederate defenses. Eventually enemy lines were less than one hundred feet apart in some places. In such close proximity for weeks on end, troops from both sides became acquainted, and passed the time shouting jokes and insults, exchanging views on the war, and trading coffee for tobacco. Those who craved excitement sometimes hung a hat on the muzzle of a rifle and raised it above the barricades to provoke the other side to shoot.

Boredom was a familiar component of each day, since there were few charges or assaults that needed to be planned and carried out, and men had little to do but listen to the heavy guns lob shells into the town. Grant himself became so overcome by monotony that he yielded to his sporadic weakness and began drinking heavily. His aides found it difficult to conceal his condition from his men.

Rather than endure such idleness, Grant's engineers began digging tunnels under the Confederates in the trenches. Their plan involved placing charges of black powder under several forts that made up part of Vicksburg's defenses, setting it off, and then sending troops through the lines during the confusion and destruction that followed. The Confederates learned of the tunneling and tried to stop it by throwing hand grenades at the work parties and then by counter mining. Those efforts failed and on June 25, Grant ordered the first explosion touched off.

The blast itself was exciting enough. It blew off the top of a hill and created a crater into which the nearby Union forces rushed. One of the besieged described the event.

Creative Corps

The Corps of Engineers was an elite and indispensable branch of the military, men whose creative talents helped the army get where it was going and protect itself when it got there. They regularly risked their lives, but took pride in their work, as historian Bruce Catton describes in *Reflections on the Civil War*.

The engineers were the part of the army that was called on when something needed to be built—roads, dams, bridges, forts, lines of entrenchments, battery emplacements, offices and living quarters at headquarters, chapels for religious services, and halls for the amateur theatricals that were relied on to sustain morale in the dull winter months. Since the army was forever needing some of these things, and now and then wanted a great many of them in a thundering hurry, the engineers were very busy people indeed. . . . When any really big project was undertaken, the engineers got help—whole regiments or even brigades from the infantry could be and very often were detailed to stack their arms, take up shovels, and go out and dig where the engineers told them to. . . .

It was the engineer officers who knew where and how things ought to be built. . . . If a bridge over a ravine had been destroyed, the engineers would bring a prefabricated bridge to the scene and put its parts together. If a stream had to be crossed that was too wide for this procedure, it was the engineers who would wheel up the great unwieldy pontoon boats and the bents, stringers, anchors, and so on that accompanied them. . . .

All in all, the engineers were kept very busy, and they got into plenty of fighting as well. It was no place for a man who believed in taking army life as easily as possible. Significantly, the engineers were a high-morale outfit, proving once more a basic fact of military life: that it is idleness and the boredom of hurry-up-and-wait that gets men down, rather than hard work and danger.

If a river was too wide to be crossed by conventional bridges, the Corps of Engineers would build pontoon bridges such as this one.

Huge masses of earth were thrown up in the air, and those who experienced it state that the ground was shook as if from an earthquake or a volcanic eruption. . . . Perceiving the fort partially destroyed, a column of the enemy's infantry, which had lain concealed in the hollow beneath the fort all day, rushed forward with loud cheers for the purpose of gaining possession of the ruins. They were gallantly met and a desperate struggle ensued. . . . So severely punished were [the Federals] in this attack that in the second attempt they made to blow up the remainder of this fort they did not try to storm the line.[108]

Grant's men exploded another mine on July 1, but it, too, did not produce the hoped-for breakthrough. The Union leader was not terribly disappointed. Vicksburg's defenders were so short of ammunition that only sharpshooters were allowed to fire at the Federals. Starvation, despair, and the big guns were breaking the town's resolve. It was only a matter of time before it would be forced to surrender.

He was right. Three days before, on June 28, Confederate general Pemberton had received from the trenches an anonymous letter that begged him to take action. "Our rations have been cut down to one biscuit and a small bit of bacon per day, not enough scarcely to keep body and soul together," it read. "Men don't want to starve and don't intend to. . . . If you can't feed us, you had better surrender us, horrible as the idea is."[109]

Pemberton, who believed that Confederate general Joseph E. Johnston was on his way to relieve the besieged town, had consulted with his staff about the possibility of resisting a little longer. Could the weakened troops fight their way out of Vicksburg if they had to? Could they stand a battle and perhaps a hard march? All but one of Pemberton's generals believed it would be impossible. The men had lived for more than a month in cramped trenches, short of food, exposed to the elements, pelted by a murderous storm of bullets, shells, and missiles. They were in no condition to walk, let alone do battle. It was time to give up the fight.

Surrender

On the morning of July 4, 1863, white flags appeared on the Confederate defenses around Vicksburg. Thousands of ragged men climbed out of their trenches, stacked their rifles, and allowed Grant's victorious Union forces to take possession of the town. Pemberton, who hailed from the North despite his Confederate sympathies, purposefully surrendered on the nation's birthday, explaining to his generals, "I know my people. I know their peculiar weaknesses and their national vanity; I know we can get better terms from them on the Fourth of July than on any other day of the year."[110]

He was partly right. In meeting with

Pemberton, Grant dealt shortly with the Confederate general's attempts to negotiate but agreed that his men be paroled—released on the condition that they not fight again—rather than sent north to prisoner of war camps. It was more of a practical than a benevolent decision. Grant believed that transporting thirty thousand men upriver would be tremendously expensive and would take months to accomplish.

Thus, Vicksburg fell, and five days later the Confederate commander of Port Hudson, one hundred miles to the south, surrendered as well. The key was in Lincoln's pocket: the Confederacy was split in two, and the Mississippi River was a Union highway again. In Lincoln's words, "The Father of Waters again goes unvexed to the sea."[111]

Grant's reaction to the momentous event was typically low-key and emotionless. "The enemy surrendered this morning,"[112] he informed the War Department in Washington. His friend Sherman, on the other hand, was elated, calling it a "day of Jubilee," and Union forces cheered when they saw the stars and stripes flying from the top of the courthouse. One Federal chaplain wrote, "The long beleaguered, stoutly defended, and sadly punished city was ours at last, and it has ever since seemed to us, who shared in the glories of that day, that we had two Fourths to celebrate. One for our

As Vicksburg's citizens look on, victorious Union troops enter their city. A U.S. flag has been hoisted over the courthouse.

national birth, and one for Vicksburg."[113]

For the citizens of Vicksburg, surrender was a bitter pill to swallow. Their pride, as well as their town, was in ruins. "Starving men, women and children with rags hanging to them stalked the streets in utter despair," one woman wrote. "They had given all for their country, and had naught left but a feeble claim on life, and this they were ready to give also but our great General Pemberton said 'No, we must give up.' "[114]

Confederate soldiers, too, found defeat hard to accept. "The members of the Third Louisiana Infantry expressed their feelings in curses loud and deep. Many broke their rifles against the trees, and scattered the ammunition over the ground where they had so long stood battling bravely and unflinchingly against overwhelming odds,"[115] wrote infantryman William H. Tunnard. It would be eighty-two years before the bitterness of defeat faded and the citizens of Vicksburg celebrated the Fourth of July again.

A Notable Victory

Vicksburg established Grant's reputation as a talented military leader, since he used a wide variety of battle techniques such as joint army-navy operations, amphibious assaults, and resourceful field engineering to conquer the well-fortified locale. While all are now common in warfare, no other Civil War general had attempted such complicated strategies. Despite the days of nonstop shelling and the terrible hardships endured, the siege was one of Grant's few victories that did not involve enormous loss of life. Fewer than five thousand Union men were killed, wounded, or missing, while Confederate casualties totaled less than three thousand.

Vicksburg marked Grant's first experiment with "total warfare," which Sherman

Generous Spirits

Although most Southerners felt enormous bitterness toward the conquerors of Vicksburg, a few residents of the city such as Willie Lord, son of the Episcopal minister, were more fair-minded in their judgment. Lord's account is included in A. A. Hoehling's *Vicksburg: 47 Days of Siege.*

In their knapsacks the men of the [Confederate] rank and file, now waifs of war, carried for the first time in many months ample rations, pressed upon them by a hospitable and admiring foe. Men who, to tantalize the starving Confederate soldiers, had shaken well-filled coffee-pots and inviting morsels . . . in grim derision, and in the face of death, across the embattled trenches, now vied [competed] with each other in seeing that their former enemy was laden with such good food and luxuries as had not been enjoyed since the capture of the well-provisioned Union camps and wagon trains at Shiloh.

This spirit of brotherly appreciation for a brave though fallen foe was reflected in the men from the qualities of their heroic leader, General Grant, who, paradoxical as it may seem, was even then a popular conquering general. He suppressed with an iron hand looting, violence and vandalism. He collected and listed all stolen goods which could be found among his men, and placarded the city and surrounding country with a proclamation calling upon all citizens who had been despoiled to call at headquarters and identify and reclaim their property. We learned this, however, too late to save our own effects. If they had been stored in the cellars of the church they would have remained intact.

At Vicksburg, Grant used amphibious assaults (pictured) and other complicated battle techniques.

1865. Both episodes produced strategic victories for the North: the fall of Vicksburg opened the Mississippi and weakened the Confederate grip on the West; the fall of Petersburg led to the surrender of both Richmond and Robert E. Lee.

Coupled with Lee's defeat at Gettysburg on July 3, the fall of Vicksburg revived the North's will to fight and sunk Southern morale to an all-time low. One month later in Richmond, Confederate general Josiah Gorgas acknowledged just what the two victories foretold:

later used with terrible effect in his sweep through Georgia. Never before in the Civil War had soldiers purposefully made war on civilians in order to hasten defeat. In this case, homes were targeted. Hospitals, even though identified by yellow flags, were not safe from artillery hits. It was a coldhearted, ungentlemanly approach, but it was effective, and Grant gained renown for his ingenuity and for his ruthlessness in war. Grant also successfully used siege tactics at Petersburg, Virginia, in

One brief month ago we were apparently at the point of success. Lee was in Pennsylvania. . . . Vicksburg seemed to laugh all Grant's efforts to scorn. . . . It seems incredible that human power could effect such a change in so brief a space. Yesterday we rode on the pinnacle of success—today, absolute ruin seems to be our portion. The Confederacy totters to its destruction.[116]

Chapter 6

Battle of Cold Harbor

On March 9, 1864, eight months after the fall of Vicksburg, President Lincoln promoted Ulysses Grant to lieutenant general, a rank previously held only by George Washington, and placed him in command of all Northern armies. As general in chief, Grant put into play a coordinated fighting strategy for the Union wherein all armies worked together to achieve victory.

His plan involved several offensives. General Benjamin "the Beast" Butler was chosen to lead an army up the James River to threaten Richmond. General Franz Sigel was put in charge of crushing opposition in the Shenandoah Valley, "the back door on Washington." General William T. Sherman was directed to march through Georgia, seize Atlanta, and lay waste the heart of the South, while General George Meade and his Army of the Potomac would go after Lee's Army of Northern Virginia. Grant himself intended to accompany Meade in order

to keep an eye on operations and foil any attempts by Lee to try to prolong the conflict. "Find out where your enemy is. Get at him as soon as you can. Strike at him as hard as you can and as often as you can, and keep moving on,"[117] he said, giving his definition of the art of war.

In May 1864, Meade's 110,000-man army set out on what would be forty of the bloodiest days of the entire war. The fighting started on May 5 in the Wilderness, a forbidding tract of land in northern Virginia, where Federal casualties tallied almost eighteen thousand and up to eleven thousand Confederates were killed or wounded. Around Spotsylvania Court House between May 8 and 19, the two armies again fought head to head and suffered almost thirty thousand casualties (Union, eighteen thousand, Confederate, twelve thousand). Neither achieved the victory for which it hoped, but Grant remained convinced that he could eventually beat the Confederates.

He was aided in that belief by fiery cavalryman Philip Sheridan, who struck a powerful blow for Union victory when he and his men shot legendary cavalry leader Jeb Stuart at Yellow Tavern on May 10, 1864. Stuart died two days later.

Lee and his sixty-thousand-man army remained a force to be reckoned with, however, and Grant set out on the night of May 20 in a southward swing around the Army of Northern Virginia, pushing toward Richmond, forcing Lee to fall back in order to protect the city.

"A Mere Question of Time"

The two armies clashed again briefly on the North Anna River from May 23 through 26, then moved south again until they were just over ten miles northeast of the Confederate capital. "We must destroy this army of Grant's before he gets to the James [River]," Lee told a staff member. "If he gets there, it will become a siege, and then it will be a mere question of time."[118]

Despite his courageous attitude, Lee and his Confederates were in poor shape for fighting. For days, the Virginian had been battling a severe intestinal disorder that plagued much of his army. Due to tragic circumstances or bad luck, the best leaders in his army were dead or in poor health. Stuart had been killed near Spotsylvania, Longstreet wounded in the Wilderness, Ewell down with dysentery made worse by exhaustion, and Hill ailing from some mysterious malady. Many

of the enlisted men were sick, and all were hungry. Some had gone without rations for two days, breaking their fast with only a slice of bacon and a biscuit or two. A great number made their marches barefoot and bleary-eyed from the nonstop fighting of the previous month. Nevertheless, the Confederates were ready to continue fighting if Lee asked them to, and he did so near Cold Harbor at the end of the month.

Maneuvering for Position

Cold Harbor, Virginia, a dusty crossroads community marked by a tumble-down tavern, was neither cold—the temperature there hovered around one hundred degrees in summer—nor located near a harbor. Some experts believe the name derived from an old English expression referring to an inn that did not serve hot meals.

The first contact between the two armies there was a cavalry skirmish on May 31. Philip Sheridan and his men clashed with Fitzhugh Lee (nephew of Robert E.) and his troops on the edge of the crossroads in the early afternoon. The two armies engaged with greater force the next day, with conditions favoring the Federals, although Lee's men put up a spirited struggle. "The whole line thundered with the incessant volleys of musketry," one New Yorker wrote. "Hundreds of our brave fellows were falling on every side."[119] At one point it appeared that Union men might push through the

Hard Skirmishing

When Ulysses Grant went on his great offensive against the Army of Northern Virginia, his men were forced to cope with grueling marches, savage battles, fear, loneliness, and fatigue. In response, many developed a tough, devil-may-care attitude that Pulitzer Prize–winning author Bruce Catton describes in *This Hallowed Ground.*

Never had armies fought like this. For a solid month they had not been out of contact. Every day, somewhere along the lines, there had been action. During this month Union losses had averaged two thousand men every single day. Old formations had been wrecked. Generals had been killed—most notable of these being [Union General] John Sedgwick, slain by a sharpshooter in the fighting at Spotsylvania Court House—and no soldier had bathed, changed his clothing, or had an unbroken night's sleep for more than four agonizing weeks. Yet morale, somehow, did not slacken; the men took what they had to take with the matter-of-fact air of old soldiers, and a New Englander in the VI Corps, noting one day that there was continuous firing going on a little way to the right, wrote casually: "I suppose it's skirmishing, as they don't call anything a battle now without the whole army is engaged and a loss of some eight or ten thousands." He added that it was hard to see what would happen to the men if this routine went on much longer—"but this army has been through so much that I don't know as you can kill them off."

Grant's soldiers endured filthy uniforms, unwashed bodies, and lack of sleep during the offensive against the Army of Northern Virginia.

Confederate line, but in spite of fewer numbers, the Southerners grimly held their ground. When one Confederate officer expressed doubt to his superior General Emory Upton that his men could continue to repel the attack, Upton snapped out, "Catch them on your bayonets and pitch them over your heads." [120]

At nightfall, both sides paused and reassessed the situation. Grant had lost heavily again and had not gained ground, but he was confident—perhaps too confident—that with an attack first thing the next morning, he could break the Confederate line. To do that, however, he needed to get his men repositioned, and to that end he sent a message to General Winfield S. Hancock to move his twenty thousand men from the extreme right of the line to the extreme left.

The order was easier given than carried out. As Hancock later explained, "Every exertion was made, but the night was dark, the heat and dust oppressive, and the roads unknown,"[121] and without adequate maps, the men took a wrong turn and got lost. They arrived the next morning, hungry, exhausted, and totally unready to take part in any immediate assault on the enemy. Reasoning that his men would fight better if they were rested and well fed, Grant decided to postpone his offensive until June 3. This tactical error gave the Confederates an extra twenty-four hours to prepare.

The Union delay allowed Lee's men, who had become experts at building defenses, time to concentrate on their earthworks. They had positioned themselves in a chain of low hills and now used the time to dig and construct a seven-mile stretch of crisscross trenches in which they could maneuver, fire on the enemy from all directions, yet be protected from at-

tack themselves. "Intricate, zig-zagged lines within lines, lines protecting flanks of lines, lines built to enfilade [fire upon] an opposing line, lines within which lies a battery, a maze and labyrinth of works within works,"[122] described one newspaper reporter who later visited the area. From the Federals' perspective, the defenses blended into the terrain so well as to appear no different than others that Lee's men had constructed. However, the ingenious fortifications, combined with Lee's skill at amassing his troops where he judged Grant would strike hardest, contributed significantly to a Union defeat the next day.

The remains of the Confederate trenches at Cold Harbor can still be seen today. Lee's men were able to ingeniously conceal the fortifications.

Premonition of Disaster

Union troops close to the front lines had watched the Confederates constructing their earthworks all day and had some idea of the defenses they would have to storm when the battle began. Because they understood that Grant would, if necessary, demand from them the ultimate sacrifice—death—to break those defenses, a great number spent an uneasy evening before the battle. Some reread letters from home or wrote to loved ones. Some "sat pale and thoughtful, forming resolutions,"[123] as one private observed.

One of Grant's staff, Colonel Horace Porter, noticed that those nearest the front lines took off their jackets and appeared to be mending them. On closer inspection, he discovered that "the men were calmly writing their names and home addresses on slips of paper and pinning them on the backs of their coats, so that their dead bodies might be recognized upon the field, and their fate made known to their families at home." One soldier went even farther, foretelling his end in his tattered diary, found later on his body on the field. "June 3. Cold Harbor. I was killed."[124]

Grant did not share this pessimism, perhaps because—as rarely happened—he did not carefully assess the task before him. First, he erroneously concluded that the South's ability and willingness to fight was on the wane. In a message he sent to Washington a week earlier, he wrote, "I feel that our success over Lee's army is already assured."[125] Second, accustomed as

he was to engaging the enemy unexpectedly and issuing instructions spur-of-the-moment as circumstances required, he failed to utilize the time he had to make extensive preparations. Neither he nor Meade examined the battlegrounds, where they might have noticed the elaborate fortifications being thrown up by the Confederates. And rather than issue a comprehensive battle plan, Meade had limited his orders to a terse, uninformative memorandum that seemed to pass most responsibilities to those lower in command. "Corps commanders will employ the interim in making examinations of the ground on their front and perfecting the arrangements for the assault."[126]

Meade's and Grant's assumption that subordinates knew what they should be doing and what was expected of them, made at least one corps leader, General William "Baldy" Smith, extremely nervous. Smith hurriedly sent a note to General Horatio Wright, the commander immediately to his left, "asking him to let me know what was to be his plan of attack, that I might conform to it, and thus have two corps acting in unison."[127] Wright responded that he was simply going to "pitch in" when the order to advance was given. Reading the reply, Smith angrily complained to his staff that the whole attack was "simply an order to slaughter my best troops."[128]

Not War, but Murder

Although he failed to clearly lay out a battle plan, Grant rightly determined to hit the enemy early and hard, and at 3:30 A.M. on June 3, three corps composed of up to sixty thousand Federals began forming into battle lines as directed by their commanders. Looking to the west, toward the Confederate entrenchments, they could see only "an apparently empty and featureless plain stretching away before them to a long line of low, flat hills."[129] It all looked innocent enough. At 4:30, with the morning mists still wreathing the hills, bugles sounded the advance, and the Federals began their charge.

The Confederates, entrenched and prepared for the attack, watched them come. "Our officers had great difficulty in restraining the men from opening fire too soon," one Confederate recalled. "But when close enough, the word 'fire' was given, and the men behind the works raised deliberately, resting their guns upon the works, and fired volley after volley."[130]

The first lines, taking the full shock of the attack, reeled and crumpled. Those who were still standing, turned and tried to retreat, but were blocked by the next column, which was advancing behind them. They had no choice but to about-face and continue their advance. As one New Hampshire man described it, "To those exposed to the full force and fury of the dreadful storm of lead and iron that met the charging column, it seemed more like a volcanic blast than a battle and was about as destructive."[131] Troops fell like dominoes hurled back against one another. The greater part of whole regiments were shot down and lay in triangle formations, their leaders dead in the lead. Some men, glancing to right

Union troops are cut down as they charge the Confederate trenches. Those who tried to retreat were blocked by columns advancing behind them.

and left, discovered that none of their comrades were still standing.

Behind their breastworks, the Confederates did not know whether to be elated or appalled by what they were accomplishing. "It was not war; it was murder,"[132] one officer remembered. The smoke was so thick that many of the enemy never saw each other at all.

In the face of such deadly fire, many Federals dropped to the ground and scooped out shallow hollows for their bodies with knives and tin dinner plates. "We piled up bodies in front of us and covering them with earth, made them serve as a defense. The dirt would sometimes sift down and expose a hand or foot, or the blackened face of the dead,"[133] one remembered. A few of the attackers actually got to the Confederate lines, but at the cost of their lives. Colonel James McMahon grabbed a flag from a wounded color-bearer and planted it on the Confederate parapet before he was shot dead, his body so riddled with bullets that he could be identified after the battle only by the distinctive buttons on his sleeves. "Heads, arms, legs, guns were seen flying high in the air," reported one Confederate artilleryman. "They closed the gaps in their line as fast as we made them, and on they came, their lines swaying like great waves of the sea."[134]

The attack itself lasted less than twenty minutes. Some Confederates were unaware that a battle had even taken place and sat waiting for the action to begin.

Grant, Meade, and Lee, who remained well behind the lines, did not receive word of the Union disaster until it was over. Meade, unaware of the state of affairs, ordered another charge, but many of his commanders refused to send their men forward from where they lay. "I will not take my regiment in another such charge if Jesus Christ himself should order it,"[135] declared a New Hampshire captain.

Fighting continued throughout the morning with the Confederates firing from behind their defenses and the Federals lying exposed in the field, shooting back as best they could. Historian Shelby Foote writes:

> Dodging shells and bullets, which continued to fall abundantly, [Federal] dispatch bearers crept forward with instructions for the assault to be renewed. The firing, most of it skyward, would swell up and then subside, until another messenger arrived with another order and the process was repeated, the men lying prone and digging in, as best they could in such cramped positions, to provide themselves with a little cover between blind volleys.[136]

At eleven o'clock Grant himself rode out to confer with his corps commanders. No one knew the full extent of the casualties, but the general consensus held that there was nothing to gain from further fighting. About one-thirty, operations were

The Color-Bearer

Although Northerners and Southerners were bitter foes during the war, many men on both sides exhibited compassion and decency to the enemy even in the midst of battle. One incident that occurred during the Union debacle of Cold Harbor is described in Noah Andre Trudeau's *Bloody Roads South.*

In front of [Confederate General] Evander Law's Alabama brigade, one Federal regiment simply melted away [were killed]—save for its color-bearer, who, unaware that there was no longer anyone behind him, steadily advanced with the flag. "Go back! Go back! We'll kill you!" some of the Alabamians shouted. But still the Union soldier came on. When he got close enough, a few Confederates even stood up and waved him away. Then, remembered an officer in the 4th Alabama, "he finally stopped, and taking the staff from its socket, rested it on the ground. He then deliberately looked, first to the right rear, and then his left rear, then seemingly for the first time taking in the situation, with the same moderation gathered in the flag, right-shouldered-shifted his charge, came to an about face as deliberately, and walked back amid the cheers of Law's men, who never saw anything equal to it before or since."

A color-bearer holds a flag battered by rifle and artillery fire during a Union advance.

suspended and the battle ground to a halt for the day.

The Killing Ground

The terrible debacle of Cold Harbor did not end on June 3, however. The dead and the wounded lay on the field under the burning sun for three days while both sides remained in battle position, lobbing shells at each other. During this time, Lee and Grant tried to reach an agreement that would allow litter-bearers and medical teams to do their work unimpeded. Lee had few wounded on the field, so had no motivation to agree to a mutual truce. He wanted Grant to ask permission for a cease-fire. Grant, on the other hand, hesitated to seek such a consideration, since it put the Union force in a subordinate position. While they negotiated, fallen Federals covered five acres of ground "as thickly as they could be laid,"[137] one general observed, and their desperate cries for help were torturous to hear. Horror-stricken troops watched one ghastly episode in which a wounded man slit his own throat with his penknife in order to end his suffering. "Calls . . . could be heard coming from the wounded and dying, and one could not sleep for the sickening sound 'W-a-t-e-r' ever sounding and echoing in his ears,"[138] said one survivor.

A burial detail gathers corpses after the battle at Cold Harbor.

Thousands died from lack of care, and the heat hurried the decomposition process. Soon the stench of decay was almost unendurable throughout the region. "The air was laden with insufferable putrescence," remembered one Federal. "We breathed it in every breath, tasted it in the food we ate and water we drank."[139] "Grant intends to *stink* Lee out of his position, if nothing else will suffice,"[140] one Richmond resident wrote. The Confederates, however, were upwind of the field and so were spared a good deal of the ordeal.

On June 7, four days after the first attack, Grant yielded to the inevitable and formally asked for a cease-fire. By then, some of the wounded had managed to crawl to safety on their own, and some had been saved by comrades who stole out on the field under cover of darkness. Only two men out of the thousands who had fallen were found alive by rescue teams. The rest had perished.

Lee's Easy Victory

While Grant and the Federals suffered agonies over their defeat, Lee and other leaders of the Confederacy celebrated their good fortune. Most division commanders reported slight losses for June 3, while others reported none at all. "[It was] perhaps the easiest victory ever granted to Confederate arms by the folly of

Breathtaking Courage

The day's battle left thousands of Union soldiers in the field, wounded and dying. Daring to risk Confederate sharpshooters poised to shoot anything that moved, Federals who had survived waited until darkness fell, then crept out to save their comrades. R. Wayne Maney describes the scene in *Marching to Cold Harbor*.

> Witnesses told of scenes of breathtaking courage as men after darkness attempted to bring in those still breathing. But the day's heat had finished the work of bullets in many cases. Many who were reached could do no more than grasp a hand and give a few words before dying. Some of those brought in lived only for a few moments after being taken to field hospitals. Slit trenches were run out to check on those with strength enough to moan, and it looked like gopher burrows radiating from the lines held by the Federal forward units. . . .
>
> With whispers and soft crawling, brave individuals tried to locate those still alive. After listening for faint breathing or moaning, they would take blankets and lift the wounded man up and noiselessly make their escape. In many cases, enlisted men would take special risks to locate the bodies of particular officers. Many of the dead were pulled back, at great risk, rather than be left on that field. . . . Soldiers searched for comrades among the dead, risking their own lives by lighting matches to identify those men on the ground.

Jefferson Davis, who had heard the artillery roar from his home in Richmond less than ten miles away.

Lee's minimal loss had been due to his reliance on field fortifications—trenches, breastworks, rifle pits, and other types of defenses—from which his men could attack as well as protect themselves in a battle. Throughout the war, Lee used entrenchments to the fullest extent, since by doing so, his relatively small force could hold off a much larger one. The principle was aptly illustrated on June 3. Confederate engineers had practiced their skills endless times. Lee's men were experts at rapid digging. Due to design and the natural layout of the land, they created a perfect killing ground at Cold Harbor.

Union casualties, when they were tallied, were appalling. Between five thousand and seven thousand Federals fell during the morning attack of June 3, most during the first fifteen minutes of fighting. Confederate casualties for that period totaled only some fifteen hundred. During the two weeks that hostilities continued, losses mounted on both sides until Federal casualties totaled about thirteen thousand, Confederate casualties about five thousand.

Butcher Grant

On June 12, with the criticism of the army and the country ringing in his ears, Grant began to move his forces out of Cold Harbor. "[This was] the greatest

Federal commanders,"[141] one colonel later wrote. "Our loss today has been small and our success, under the blessing of God, all that we could expect,"[142] Lee wrote to and most inexcusable slaughter of the whole war,"[143] wrote one New Hampshire soldier. "I am disgusted with the generalship displayed. Our men have, in many cases, been foolishly and wantonly sacrificed,"[144] a New Yorker complained to his sister. "Grant is a butcher and not fit to be at the head of an army," Mary Lincoln stated.

Mary Lincoln had little respect for Grant, calling him a butcher of men.

"He loses two men to the enemy's one. He has no *management*, no regard for life. . . . I could fight an army as well myself."[145]

The Confederates dubbed Cold Harbor "Grant's slaughter pen."[146] The battle went down in the pages of history as one of the most destructive and profitless engagements of the Civil War, as well as one of Grant's worst misjudgments. "I regret this assault more than any one I ever ordered,"[147] he said on the evening of June 3. The remark shocked his staff, who had never before heard him admit a mistake.

The fiasco did not shake the general's confidence, however, and true to a promise he had made to Lincoln after the Battle of the Wilderness, he did not retreat. In his mind, there was no need to. His strategic advantage over Lee still held. The Virginian was weakened. He had used up valuable manpower and supplies and could no longer make offensive thrusts as he had early in the war. In fact, he could do nothing but retreat if he wanted to protect Richmond.

But four bloody head-to-head attacks had yielded Grant too little profit. He had lost more than fifty thousand men since the beginning of May, a number equal to half the casualties suffered by the Army of the Potomac since the beginning of the war. (Lee had lost twenty-seven thousand, almost half of his army.) The Federals were battered and exhausted. Union reinforcements from the North could and did make up lost numbers, but even as large a force as the Army of the

Potomac could not take such a pounding for long and survive.

Thus the tenacious, versatile Union general opted for a change of plan. Instead of battling his way to the doors of Richmond, he decided to proceed on a more roundabout route, by way of Petersburg. The siege he instituted there lasted ten months before the Confederate railroad hub and supply depot fell into Federal hands. In the meantime, William T.

Although the Union army replaced the troops lost at Cold Harbor, Grant's forces could not survive any further punishment of that scale.

Sherman began his offensive against Atlanta and the South. "I can make Georgia howl,"[148] the lean, redheaded fighter promised Grant. Georgia and the Carolinas were about to feel the effects of all-out war, and it would prove to be a deathblow to the Confederacy.

Chapter 7

Sherman's March

I n May 1864, while Ulysses Grant and Robert E. Lee clashed repeatedly from the Wilderness to Cold Harbor, Union general William Tecumseh Sherman and an army of almost one hundred thousand men set out from Chattanooga, Tennessee, on what would be a yearlong march through the South. Grant, general-in-chief of all Union armies, had chosen his trusted friend and most capable subordinate to carry out part of the North's "grand offensive"—the coordinated effort of all Union armies to win the war.

Grant directed Sherman "to move against [Confederate general Joseph] Johnston's army, break it up, and get into the interior of the enemy's country as far as you can, inflicting all the damage you can against their war resources."[149] In other words, Sherman was not only to destroy Johnston's army, he was to wage war on those who supported the rebellion as well. He would disrupt transportation

and communication systems, destroy factories and fields, and confiscate private property. "We are not only fighting armies, but a hostile people, and must make old and young, rich and poor, feel the hard hand of war,"[150] Sherman declared.

The First Objective

Sherman, a native Ohioan who had trained at the U.S. Military Academy at West Point, was familiar with the South, since he had served as the first superintendent of a Louisiana military academy (later to become Louisiana State University) just prior to the war. He had foreseen the terrible toll the war would take on the country and had suffered a nervous breakdown in late 1861 while guarding the Kentucky border against Confederates. Recovering, he had been assigned to serve under Grant in Tennessee, and the general's friendship and trust had brought out the best in Sherman. The Ohioan took over his friend's command of the armies of the West when Grant became general in chief.

Given his new assignment, Sherman's first objective was to prepare his troops for the long campaign. A practical man who had no time to waste on formalities such as discipline, manners, well-kept uniforms, and polished boots, he concentrated instead on everything that his army would need to achieve its ends. Work crews were trained to repair railroad tracks, build bridges, create roads, and string communication wires in record time. Wagons carried prefabricated canvas pontoons that could be thrown across rivers to make bridges. Telegraph operators carried their own equipment, and engineers had their own wagons in which to prepare maps of the region through which the army would be passing. So many supplies were stockpiled at Nashville, Tennessee, one of the army's supply

In preparation for his march, Union general William T. Sherman trained work crews to repair railroad tracks (below) and string communication wires (right).

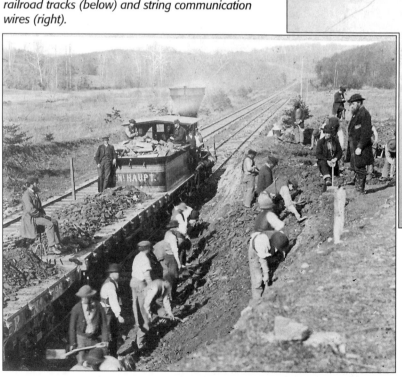

bases, that it was described as "one vast storehouse—warehouses covering city blocks, one a quarter of a mile long; stables by the ten and twenty acres, repair shops by the fieldful."[151]

Despite such attention to detail, Sherman planned to travel fast and light and to threaten anyone who might slow the march. Historian Shelby Foote writes, "[He was] a violent-talking man whose bite at times measured up to his bark."[152] Yet his men loved and respected him, probably because he genuinely cared for them and was never pompous or arrogant. Restless, untidy, irritable, and full of enormous energy, he was always on the move, slept little, and talked nonstop. One visitor to his camp wrote, "At his departure I felt it a relief, and experienced almost an exhaustion after the excitement of his vigorous presence."[153]

Kennesaw Mountain

Joseph E. Johnston, the Confederate commander Sherman was pursuing, was as popular with his men as was his Federal counterpart. Fifty-four years old in 1861, he had helped win the First Battle of Bull Run and was a veteran of almost every other major campaign of the war. "I do not believe there was a soldier in his army but would gladly have died for him," wrote Confederate Sam Watkins. "With him, everything was his soldiers. . . . He would feed his soldiers if the country starved."[154]

Johnston, poorly supplied and with only sixty thousand men, was determined to keep the Yankees away from Atlanta, and he blocked the Union army's path every chance he got. One particularly vigorous engagement occurred on June 27 at Kennesaw Mountain, when thirteen thousand of Sherman's men assaulted the well-entrenched Confederates who were above them in the hills. In one particularly deadly attack in a locale later dubbed "the Dead Angle," wave after wave of Federals advanced up a slope only to be shot down, bayoneted, or captured. Confederate Sam Watkins, who fought in the battle wrote:

> I've heard men say that if they ever killed a Yankee during the war they were not aware of it. I am satisfied that on this memorable day, every man in our regiment killed from . . . twenty to a hundred each. All that was necessary was to load and shoot. Afterward, I heard a soldier say he thought "hell had broke loose in Georgia, sure enough."[155]

Federal casualties at Kennesaw Mountain totaled three thousand in comparison to eight hundred for the Confederates. Sherman never admitted that the attack had been a mistake, but in following weeks he returned to more successful flanking maneuvers, whereby his men marched around the Confederates, attacking from the side, forcing Johnston to fall back. "You-uns swing around on your ends like a gate," said one Confederate. "Sherman'll never go to hell. He'll flank the devil and make heaven despite the guards,"[156] said another.

On to Atlanta

Although Sherman's directive was to break up Joe Johnston's army, another of his primary objectives was to capture Atlanta, symbol of Southern resistance and railroad hub and manufacturing center for the Confederacy. Its fall would go far toward demoralizing the South, and would make supplying Southern armies with food and war matériel even more difficult.

By mid-July, the two armies were in sight of Atlanta, and residents were nervous despite the miles of defenses that protected the city from easy invasion. A stream of refugees from the countryside, fleeing the oncoming Yankees, daily swelled the population. Parks sprouted row upon row of hospital tents full of wounded; coffin makers could not keep up with orders; and those citizens with money bought seats on southbound trains out of town. "This place is to the Confederacy as important as the heart is to the body," Georgia governor Joseph E. Brown wrote to Jefferson Davis. "We must hold it."[157]

Jefferson Davis agreed, but he was skeptical of Johnston's ability to hold back the Federals, afraid that he would give up Atlanta without a fight. Thus, on July 17, 1864, he abruptly removed the much loved Johnston from command, replacing him with General John Bell Hood, who was a renowned warrior but whose men had nicknamed him "Old Woodenhead." "Hood is a bold fighter," Lee himself said, "I am doubtful as to other qualities necessary."[158] Johnston's men were devastated by the order. "Farewell, old fellow! We privates loved

Southern refugees flee Sherman's advancing forces. Sherman was determined to wage all-out war on Confederate soldiers and civilians alike.

you because you made us love ourselves,"[159] one wrote in his journal. "This act threw a damper over this army from which it never recovered,"[160] another remembered.

Sherman on the other hand, was delighted at the news. He was convinced that if Hood tried to force a fight, he could be defeated. True to form, on July 20, Hood struck Sherman's army hard at Peachtree Creek, north of the city in front of the Confederate defenses. Sherman beat back the attack. Hood then rushed his men east of the city to attempt to stop Union general James B. McPherson and his army from cutting rail lines to Richmond. The two armies clashed in what would be known as the Battle of Atlanta, and McPherson, a likable and gifted leader whom Sherman predicted would someday outshine Grant, was shot and killed. Grief stricken, Sherman nevertheless retained his focus and substituted General John "Black Jack" Logan, who spurred his men forward with cries of "McPherson and revenge, boys, McPherson and revenge."[161] Their counterattack was so strong that Hood's men were driven from the field in less than thirty minutes, eventually taking refuge in Atlanta itself.

"This Flame-Wrapped City"

Rather than continue assaulting the city's defenses at the cost of thousands of lives, Sherman sealed off the town and began

Sherman reviews one of his cannon crews prior to the shelling of Atlanta.

shelling it heavily. "Another week of anxiety and suspense . . . and the fate of Atlanta is still undecided," wrote an Atlanta merchant. "It is like living in the midst of a pestilence. No one can tell but he may be the next victim."[162]

The siege went on for five weeks, at the end of which time, Sherman's troops managed to cut the last supply line into the city. On September 1, Hood and his men evacuated Atlanta, and Sherman and his men occupied it the next day. "Atlanta is ours and fairly won,"[163] he telegraphed to Washington. Outside Petersburg, Ulysses S. Grant took a moment from directing his own siege to order a one-hundred-gun salute to be fired in Sherman's honor. "I feel you have accomplished the most gigantic undertaking given to any general in this war," he wrote to his friend. "It gives me as much pleasure to record this in your favor as it would in favor of any living man, myself included."[164]

With Atlanta under his control, Sherman began making plans for its destruction. Foundry, freight warehouses, slave markets, and businesses were all slated to be burned. He planned to spare private homes, but civilians were told to evacuate, just in case. "If the people raise a howl against my barbarity and cruelty, I will answer that war is war and not popularity-seeking. If they want peace they and their relatives must stop war,"[165] he explained to a Washington official.

On November 15, his men set fire to the city in a never-to-be-forgotten conflagration. "All the pictures and verbal descriptions of hell I have ever seen never gave me half so vivid an idea of it as did this flame-wrapped city tonight,"[166] remembered one of Sherman's staff. By dawn, a third of the city was rubble and smoking ashes.

A Gigantic Pleasure Excursion

While fires still burned in Atlanta, Sherman set off on the next leg of his mission, marching his army through the heart of Georgia to the coast. The purpose would be "total warfare"—destroying not only the Confederate government and military but civilian support systems as well. It was a relatively uncommon approach, since most military men believed that war

The ruins of Atlanta show the damage wrought by Sherman's troops. Fires set on November 15 destroyed a third of the city.

should be waged between armies, not on innocent women and children. Grant supported Sherman's vision, but worried that the Federals would be unable to maintain themselves during the long trip. They would be isolated, surrounded by hostiles, miles from fellow armies. If they came under severe attack, there would be no one to come to the rescue.

Sherman was insistent, however. He faced only minimum danger, since most of Georgia's men were out of state, fighting with their regiments. Those who remained were poorly trained or too old or too young to be truly effective. The Federals numbered sixty-two thousand strong (Sherman had sent a large portion of his force under the command of General George Thomas back to Tennessee to hold the state against Confederate assault). They could avoid heavy population centers where there might be serious armed resistance. They would stick to the countryside and concentrate on plantations and farms that provided supplies to the Confederate army. "The utter destruction of [Georgia's] roads, houses and people will cripple their military resources," he pointed out, and "if the North can march an army right through the South, it is proof positive that the North can prevail."[167]

Sherman did not plan to give his men permission to ruthlessly rape, murder, and pillage. He did, however, plan for them to live off the land, and regular foraging parties, the "bummers," were as-

Spoils of War

Sherman officially prohibited his men from looting civilians during the march through the South, but reality was different from policy, as Shelby Foote explains in *The Civil War, A Narrative.*

> Isolated plantation owners, mostly wives and mothers whose sons and husbands were with Hood or Lee in Tennessee or Virginia, buried their silver and jewels on hearing of Sherman's approach, and the search for these provided fun, as well as the possibility of profit, for the blue-clad visitors. Out would come the ramrods for a vigorous probing of lawns and flowerbeds. "It was comical to see a group of these red-bearded, barefooted, ragged veterans punching the unoffending earth in an apparently idiotic but certainly most energetic way," an officer who observed them was to write. "A woman standing upon the porch of a house, watching their proceedings, instantly became an object of suspicion, and she was watched until some movement betrayed a place of concealment. Fresh earth thrown up, a bed of flowers just set out, the slightest indication of a change in appearance or position, all attracted the gaze of these military agriculturists. If they 'struck a vein' a spade was instantly put in requisition and the coveted wealth was speedily unearthed. It was all fair spoil of war, and the search made one of the excitements of the march."

signed the task of collecting food for men and animals. "Soldiers must not enter the dwellings of inhabitants or commit any trespass,"[168] Sherman reminded everyone in his orders. Nevertheless, once into the march his men stole jewelry, silver, and

furniture; carried off animals; and burned barns, fields, fences, and homes. One woman remembered:

Believing they hear the sounds of approaching Confederates, Union "bummers" pause in their search for food.

> Like Demons they rushed in! . . . To my Smoke House, my dairy, pantry, kitchen and cellar, like famished wolves they come, breaking locks and whatever is in their way. The thousand pounds of meat in my smoke house is gone . . . my flour, my meat, my lard, butter, eggs, pickles . . . wine, jars and jugs are all gone. My 18 fat turkeys, my hens, chickens, and fowl, my young pigs, are shot down in my yard . . . as if they were the rebels themselves.[169]

"This is probably the most gigantic pleasure excursion ever planned," one veteran

declared. "It already beats everything I ever saw soldiering, and promises to prove much richer yet."[170] Sherman ignored the damage they wrought, calling it exceptional and incidental, and pointed out that, if Southern civilians were treated roughly, their support for the war would be weakened. In fact, they would be more likely to urge their men to stop fighting and return home to protect them.

Many Confederate soldiers did desert after receiving letters from wives and mothers that told of Sherman's marauding. One such letter read: "Try to get off and come home and fix us all up some. . . . If you put off a-coming, 'twont be no use to come, for we'll all hands of us be out there in the garden in the graveyard with your ma and mine."[171] So widespread were the desertions that Jefferson Davis remarked, "Sherman's campaign has produced bad effects on our people. Success against his future operations is needful to animate public confidence."[172]

There was little that could be done, however. Sherman's army was a vast, well-oiled marching machine that swept a - fifty-mile path through the countryside, marching ten to fifteen miles a day, creating roads and bridges whenever necessary, ripping up and twisting railroad tracks into shapes dubbed "Sherman's neckties," destroying everything in their path. "They say no living thing is found in Sherman's track," wrote one Southern woman, "only chimneys, like telegraph poles, to carry the news of (his) attack backwards."[173]

True to Sherman's predictions, his men encountered little fighting between Atlanta and the Atlantic. One of the few infantry clashes took place as they circled past Macon, Georgia. Armed troops defending the town marched out to meet the Federals on November 22. As they approached the hill on which fifteen hundred of Sherman's men were positioned, the Confederates broke into a run and charged across the fields with "more courage than discretion,"[174] according to one Federal. A heavy blast of rifle fire sent them retreating, but they quickly reformed their ranks and charged again. After a third attempt and a third repulse, the survivors retreated back into town, leaving Union troops free to inspect the battlefield. When they did, they discovered to their horror that they had been fighting old men and young boys, whose faces showed the fear and agony they suffered as

Union troops destroy farms and railroad tracks in their advance through the South. Sherman felt that such devastation would weaken civilian support of the war.

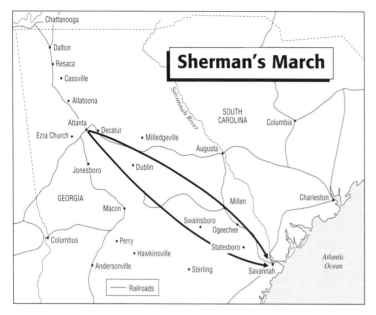

Sherman's March

they died. More than six hundred Confederates lay dead, while only sixty Federals had been killed. "I was never so affected at the sight of dead and wounded before," wrote one Illinois soldier. "I hope we will never have to shoot at such men again. They knew nothing at all about fighting and I think their officers knew as little."[175]

Saviors and Sufferers

Armed troops did little to slow Sherman's progress, but thousands of Negroes who flocked to his camps and followed his columns, caused him continual concern. Most of these ex-slaves—men, women, and children of all ages—feared being caught by Confederates and returned to slavery, and so stayed close to the Federals, whom they saw as saviors and protectors. "[They followed the army] like a

sable cloud in the sky, . . ." one officer wrote. "They thought it was freedom now or never."[176]

Sherman, who shared many Americans' racist attitudes, grew impatient with these followers and explained repeatedly to their leaders that he "wanted the slaves to remain where they were, and not load us down with useless mouths which would eat up the food needed for our fighting men."[177] Some listened. Some grew so tired that they turned back. In one instance, a number dropped out after finding several abandoned plantations, which they took over and began to farm. Many, however, persisted in following the army, determined to get to the North or die in the attempt.

Such was the case in one tragic incident that occurred near Ebenezer Creek, thirty miles from Savannah, on December 3. One of Sherman's more reckless subordinates, General Jefferson C. Davis of Indiana, was hurrying the last of his men across a temporary pontoon bridge, away from pursuing Confederates, when he thought of a way of cutting off the hundreds of refugees who were tailing his column. As soon as the last soldier was across, Davis ordered his engineers to take up the pontoons. The Negroes were stranded on the other side. The sound of approaching horsemen drove them to act, however. Desperately, they plunged into the icy water, those in the rear pushing and shoving those in the front. As Confederates arrived and began shooting, the push became a stampede. Women, children, and old people were trampled. Many who could not swim drowned.

Prisoners of War

While marching across Georgia, William Sherman and his men were horrified to stumble across several Federal escapees from Andersonville, one of the most notorious Southern prison camps of the war. Both the North and South maintained such camps, which held about 400,000 soldiers altogether. Conditions in most were nightmarish as Geoffrey Ward describes in *The Civil War, An Illustrated History*.

> At Libby Prison . . . in Richmond, six dank rooms held thirteen hundred Union officers, while at Belle Isle in the James [River], 90 percent of the survivors weighed less than one hundred pounds. "Can those be *men*?" asked Walt Whitman when he saw several prisoners returned from Belle Isle: ". . . Are they not really mummied, dwindled corpses? They lay there, most of them, quite still, but with a horrible look in their eyes. . . ."
>
> Smallpox killed eighteen hundred Confederates at Rock Island, Illinois, and there were never enough blankets for all the southerners at Elmira, New York. . . . Food was in short supply, too: "Five chews of tobacco would buy a rat, a rat would buy five chews of tobacco, a loaf of bread would buy a rat, a rat would buy a loaf of bread. . . ."
>
> The worst was Andersonville in Georgia. . . . Its commandant, a temperish German-Swiss immigrant named Henry Wirz, forbade prisoners to build shelters; most lived in holes scratched in the ground, covered by a blanket. . . . Each inmate's daily ration was a teaspoon of salt, three tablespoons of beans, and half a pint of unsifted cornmeal. A foul trickle called Sweet Water Branch served as both drinking water and sewer. Thirteen thousand men died at Andersonville and were buried in mass graves; on one day they died at the rate of a man every eleven minutes.

This skeletal Union soldier is a survivor of the notorious Andersonville prison camp.

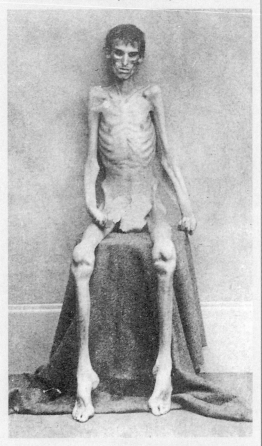

Davis's troops turned back to give what help they could, but for some of the least fortunate it was too late. One soldier later wrote, "There were many . . . to whom it was literally preferable to die freemen rather than to live slaves."[178]

"A Christmas Gift"

The tragedy at Ebenezer Creek went almost unnoticed in the North, since Sherman had cut off communications shortly after leaving Atlanta, and no one—including Grant and Lincoln—had any notion of his progress. "Sherman's army is now somewhat in the condition of a ground-mole when he disappears under a lawn," said Grant. "You can here and there trace his track, but you are not quite certain where he will come out until you see his head."[179]

Then in late December, Sherman reappeared on the Georgia coast and captured Savannah. Compared with his struggles to take Atlanta, it was an easy undertaking. Less than ten thousand troops were stationed in the city; far fewer than would be needed to halt Sherman's march. Officers judged it wiser to evacuate and join forces with other Confederate troops in the Carolinas than to resist. Thus, on December 20, they quietly withdrew northward across a hastily completed, makeshift bridge, leaving the city to looters and Sherman's men. The red-haired general promptly sent a telegraph to Abraham Lincoln. "I beg to present you, as a Christmas gift, the city of Savan-nah, with one hundred fifty heavy guns and plenty of ammunition; also, about 25,000 bales of cotton."[180]

The Smoky March

Sherman's men spent a month in Savannah, then, ignoring the winter weather, they started north into the Carolinas. Confederate leaders were certain that the enormous army could not drag itself, its three thousand wagons, and its heavy artillery through calf-deep mud and heavy rain, but the train managed to cover ten miles a day, with battalions of men hacking down forests to build corduroy roads (logs laid crosswise) where necessary. When one Federal was injured stepping on a land mine that had been buried previously, Sherman forced Confederate prisoners to march ahead of his columns with picks and shovels to ensure the army's safety. The prisoners protested that they did not know where the explosives lay, but Sherman did not relent. "I don't care a damn if *you're* blown up!" he replied. "I'll not have my own men killed like this."[181]

Sherman and his men had been ruthless in Georgia, but they were even harsher in South Carolina. "Here is where treason *began* and, by God, here is where it shall end!"[182] cried one soldier. In what became known as the Smoky March, Sherman's men burned and pillaged with greater enthusiasm than ever before. Barns and homes were plundered, then set afire. Split-rail fences smoked and crackled along the roadsides. Small towns and villages along the way were stripped of goods.

The army arrived in Columbia, the state capital, on February 17, 1865, and the destruction became proportionately greater as troops celebrated by looting liquor stores and setting fire to buildings and bales of cotton left behind when Confederates fled. (Sherman later claimed that retreating Confederates set the fires themselves.) A brisk winter wind spread the flames until entire blocks were on fire. "All around us were falling . . . showers of burning flakes. Everywhere the palpitating blaze walled the streets as far as the eye could reach, filling the air with its terrible roar," wrote one young girl, from a position near the town's center. "On every side (was) the crackling and devouring fire, while every instant came the crashing of timbers and the thunder of falling buildings. A quivering molten ocean seemed to fill the air and sky." [183]

Sherman himself tried to control his men, but there was little that could be done. By morning, the city was rubble. "Though I never ordered it, and never wished it, I have never shed any tears over [the burning]," Sherman said. "I believe that it hastened what we all fought for—the end of the war." [184]

Two days later, on February 20, the Federals moved out of Columbia and resumed their march north. Most of the army was delighted with what they had effected in the state, but at least one soldier felt some sympathy for its citizens. "South Carolina may have been the cause of the whole thing," he wrote, "but she has had an awful punishment." [185]

Beating Joe Johnston

Sherman reached North Carolina, where his men set fire to pine forests and demolished weapons arsenals. There he learned that Joseph Johnston had been placed in command of Confederate forces in the Carolinas, to try and slow the Federal push there. In mid-March, Johnston went on the offensive at Bentonville, thirty-five miles south of Raleigh, attacking Sherman's force with just twenty thousand troops,

The burned-out buildings of Columbia, South Carolina, after Sherman's men looted its stores and set fire to buildings and bales of cotton.

many of whom were mere boys. One group of Junior Reserves, led by seventeen-year-old Major Walter Clark, "repulsed every charge that was made upon them,"[186] as one of their superiors proudly testified. In heavy fighting, the Confederates lost more than twenty-five hundred men, killed and wounded, and were forced to retreat. "Sherman's course cannot be hindered by the small force I have," Johnston wired to Lee. "I can do no more than annoy him."[187]

Sherman, who later admitted that he had let slip the opportunity to crush Johnston's army at Bentonville, allowed his men a brief, well-earned rest near Goldsboro, North Carolina, shortly after the battle. Since leaving Savannah, they had covered more than four hundred miles of muddy roads, plunged through swamps, forded rivers, and fended off Confederate attacks. The hardships had turned them into scarecrows—tired, thin, and dressed in tatters. Historian Burke Davis describes:

> It was an absurd caricature of an army, with hardly a complete uniform in its ranks. Half the men were barefoot or wore wrappings of old blankets or quilts. Socks had disappeared months before. There was a sprinkling of rebel uniforms, and thousands were in civilian clothes— battered silk top hats, cutaway coats and tightlegged breeches of the Revolutionary era. Some wore women's bonnets. . . . Faces were still smudged from pine smoke and gunpowder. Lank

hair protruded from ruined hats; many of the hatless wore handkerchiefs around their heads. Hundreds were without shirts, bare to the waist.[188]

The army set out again around the tenth of April, moving northwest toward Raleigh. Their march was broken when a courier arrived with the news that Lee had surrendered to Grant at Appomattox Court House, Virginia, on April 9. Raleigh, the capital of North Carolina, capitulated to the Federals on April 12, and on April 17 Sherman and Johnston met near Durham, northeast of the capital, to arrange Johnston's own terms of surrender. Sherman expressed his desire to "save the people of North Carolina the damage they would sustain by the march of this army through the central or western parts of the state,"[189] and proposed the same terms Grant had offered Lee the week before. Johnston agreed and formally surrendered on April 26. The war, for all intents and purposes, was over.

"The Rebels Are Whipped to Death"

Sherman's march resulted in hundreds of miles of burned countryside, millions of dollars of lost property and goods, and the end of plantation society, which had been the pride of the South. His men burned fifteen towns, including two major cities (Atlanta and Columbia); captured at least two others (Raleigh and Savannah); overwhelmed Johnston's army; and skirmished with endless Confederates along the way. As a result of the ruthlessness of their behavior, a legacy of hatred was born, particularly among Southern women, that would last for generations.

In military terms, Sherman's march undoubtedly hastened the end of the war and helped bring the South to its knees. His capture of Atlanta was the good news that boosted Northern morale and undoubtedly helped ensure Lincoln's reelection in November 1864. Sherman's practice of destroying civilian property and public morale killed the last vestiges of Southern support for the war and brought the conflict to a long-overdue end.

The march also made Sherman's reputation as a brilliant strategist who attained his military objectives quickly and efficiently. Although many saw him as a man of violence—a despot who took pleasure in giving pain to his enemies—the relatively bloodless campaign he conducted across the South attested to the priority he put on hastening the war's end and preserving lives.

General Lee surrenders to General Grant at Appomattox Court House on April 9, 1865.

I confess, with shame, I am sick and tired of fighting—its glory is all moonshine; even success most brilliant is over dead and mangled bodies . . . and it is only those who have never heard a shot, never heard the shrieks and groans of the wounded and lacerated . . . that cry aloud for more blood, more vengeance, more desolation. I *know* the rebels are whipped to death, and I declare before God, as a man and a soldier, I will not strike a foe who stands unarmed and submissive before me, but would rather say—"Go and sin no more."[190]

Chapter 8

Battle for Restoration

The Civil War ended on April 9, 1865, when Confederate general Robert E. Lee surrendered his Army of Northern Virginia to Ulysses S. Grant at Appomattox Court House, Virginia. During their historic meeting, Grant was generous in his treatment of his former enemy, doing his best to put Lee at his ease, promising to provide food and supplies to the hungry Confederates and allowing them to keep their horses, which could be used in planting crops that summer. Lee was equally gracious in defeat. "This will have a very happy effect on my army,"[191] he said after reading the terms of surrender Grant had offered.

The civility that existed between the two leaders was seen less often between Northerner and Southerner in following years. The war was over, but its repercussions were only beginning. During the next turbulent twelve-year period—known as Reconstruction—conflicts again arose over differences in vision.

Some men wanted a quick reunion of the nation and the renewal of former social and economic relationships between the North and South. Others saw a need to punish the South for its rebellion and to forcibly ensure that former slaves were granted equal rights. Such irreconcilable points of view quickly evolved into dissension and discord, which both slowed the process of healing and worsened the division between North and South immeasurably.

Dispute over Terms

As early as December 1863, while the war still raged, Abraham Lincoln drew up his own plan for reconstruction. He proposed quickly bringing the South back into the Union under lenient and generous terms. He supported pardoning every Southerner (high-ranking officers excepted) who would take an oath of loyalty to the United States, uphold the abolition of slavery, and agree to protect and defend the Constitution. When 10 percent of a state's voters (based on the 1860 election) had taken such an oath, they could set up a state government and be recognized as a part of the Union again. The status of blacks was left undefined. Details such as those would be worked out in the future. When critics pointed out that his policy was extremely lenient, Lincoln explained that it was only a jumping-off point for further reforms. "Concede that the new government . . . is only to what it should be as the egg is to the fowl, we shall sooner have a fowl by hatching the egg than by smashing it." [192]

Many Congressional Republicans, known as Radicals because of their immoderate, hard-line approach to political issues, outspokenly disagreed with Lincoln. Two of the most radical, Congressman Henry Winter Davis of Maryland and Senator Ben Wade of Ohio, proposed their own bill. It called for military gover-

nors to rule Confederate states until new constitutions could be drawn up; required 50 percent of each state's voters to take the loyalty oath before that state could rejoin the Union; and prevented anyone from voting who had willingly supported the Confederacy. The last would have denied the vote to hundreds of thousands of Southern men. Lincoln believed the Wade-Davis bill to be too harsh and killed it with what came to be known as a pocket veto—he stuffed it into his pocket and thereafter ignored it.

The crisis passed, but the battle was just beginning. If Lincoln had lived, he might have carried enough influence to push through his plan when the war ended, but on April 15, 1865, five days after Lee's surrender to Grant, the president

Free blacks set up camp outside Richmond, Virginia, after the war. The status of blacks was left undefined in Abraham Lincoln's plan for reconstruction.

War's Aftermath

The South lay desolate after the war. Cities, farms, and plantations were in ruins. Livestock, crops, industry, and transportation systems were destroyed. The effect of such destruction was personally devastating as well, as Richard W. Murphy describes in *The Nation Reunited, War's Aftermath*.

People scrabbled for a living in any way they could. Landowners who had never held a job took positions as clerks and farmhands or joined the crews laboring to repair the ruined railroads. The New York *Tribune*'s James Shepherd Pike came across a ramshackle South Carolina mansion occupied by the sole survivor of one of the richest families in the state. Pike reported that the man earned his living peddling "tea by the pound and molasses by the quart, on a corner of the old homestead, to the former slaves of the family."

Anarchy was everywhere . . . with "villages sacked in Yankee style by lawless mobs, and every man returning from the army on mule or horse having to guard his animals & himself with loaded weapons." . . . Loathing of the North was widespread and unrelenting. A Savannah woman taught her children never to utter the word "Yankee" without adding the epithets "hateful" and "thieving." A North Carolina innkeeper told a Northern journalist that the Yankees had killed his sons, burned his house and stolen his slaves, leaving him only with the privilege of venting his spleen [anger]: "I git up at half-past four in the morning, and sit up till twelve at night, to hate 'em."

was assassinated by John Wilkes Booth, an actor and disgruntled white supremacist. Vice President Andrew Johnson, a Demo-

crat and conservative with, as historian Bruce Catton describes, "a genius for making enemies and estranging friends,"[193] assumed office. The new president had a great deal of sympathy for slavery and states' rights, and he did not particularly want to punish the South or restructure Southern society. Rather he hoped to restore the Union, help the South rebuild, and then allow events to take their course.

Black Codes

Under Johnson's plan, set forth in May 1865, virtually all Southerners were pardoned, and defeated states only had to agree to abolish slavery and support the Union before they were allowed to form new governments. The status of blacks was all but ignored—individual states were to determine their own civil rights policies. Delighted with such generous terms, Southern states began reorganizing almost immediately. When elections were held, winners were usually racially biased in their outlook and promptly passed legislation known as Black Codes. These codes sharply restricted the social, political and economic rights of blacks and allowed discriminatory behavior against them. Some codes stated that blacks could not own weapons, could not live within town limits unless they worked for a white person, could not preach or do business without special permits. Some set restrictions on occupations that blacks could hold and property they could own. Others allowed black children to be hired out to work or bound as apprentices to white employers. In fact, blacks were emancipated, but they were still under the thumb of their oppressors. One Southerner wrote, "The Negroes are no more free than they were forty years ago, and if anyone goes about the country telling them that they are free, shoot him."[194]

The Black Codes dismayed Northerners and produced further tension between the two sections of the country, and that tension heightened as time passed.

From Outrage to Impeachment

When Congress convened in December 1865, Radical Republicans were outraged over Johnson's plan and quickly took steps to ensure that Union victory stood for something more than just a restoration of the "old South." They refused to recognize the legitimacy of new Southern governments and barred Southern representatives from taking their seats in Congress. In early 1866 they passed the Civil Rights Act, which guaranteed various legal rights for former slaves, and the Fourteenth Amendment (ratified in 1868), designed to give citizenship to blacks and to guarantee that all federal and state laws applied equally to blacks and whites alike. Several Reconstruction Acts, passed in 1867, divided the South into five military districts, each headed by a commander who oversaw voter registration of both blacks and whites, supervised the forma-

tion of conventions to adopt new state constitutions, and ensured that the Fourteenth Amendment was ratified before the state rejoined the Union.

Johnson stubbornly vetoed most of these bills, but the powerful Congress overrode his veto and even instituted impeachment proceedings against him in 1868, citing that he committed "high crimes and misdemeanors" by obstructing implementation of their Reconstruction policy. After a trial that lasted more than ten weeks, Johnson was acquitted by a single vote.

Military Occupation

Radical Reconstruction, as it came to be called, made Southerners once again feel like they were occupied by the enemy. Only twenty thousand Federal soldiers, sent to maintain order, were stationed

Tickets like this one were issued for attendance to the impeachment proceedings against President Johnson. Johnson was acquitted by one vote.

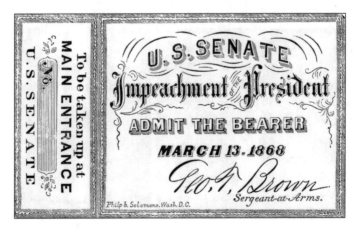

After the war, Richmond, Virginia, is occupied by Federal troops. White Southerners resented the soldiers' presence, as can be seen by these ladies' expressions.

Society seemed to be turned topsy-turvy, since Southerners who cooperated with Federal mandates increased their power and affluence while those who did not—including formerly wealthy slave- and landowners—remained powerless and struggled to make ends meet. Particularly infuriating for many whites was the necessity of watching former slaves taking advantage of their newfound freedoms—voting (for males only), going to school in some of the nation's first free public schools, even making their way into public office. "Bottom rail on top!" [196] one black man exulted, when Hiram Revels, a free black, educated at Knox College in Illinois, was elected to Jefferson Davis's former seat in the U.S. Senate in 1870.

Terrorism and Violence

Angry and frustrated, some who were deprived of their possessions and embittered over losing the war lashed out against those whom they saw as inferior, ignorant, or corrupt. They formed secret organizations such as the Knights of the White Camellia, the Sons of Midnight, and the Ku Klux Klan, which were allegedly designed to protect the weak, the innocent, and the defenseless and to safeguard and defend the Constitution of the United States. In reality such groups were agencies of intimidation. Members donned robes and hooded masks in attempts to

throughout the South, but Southerners reacted to their presence with fear and bitterness. One woman wrote, "Oh, my God, when will the dark days end which seem [to be] enveloping our stricken land in deeper gloom, day by day," and another declared "an almost unlimited military despotism is holding the south as conquered territory and despair is laying its icy hand on all." [195] Almost as galling as the soldiers were Northern civilians (known as carpetbaggers, since they carried their goods in suitcases) who flocked south to aid and educate blacks or to buy cheap land and property and make their fortunes.

frighten blacks and public officials and to keep them from voting, holding office, or exercising their political rights. When nonviolent tactics failed, members resorted to beatings, torture, and murder to achieve their ends. A black man could be whipped for not lifting his hat to a white man or be lynched for attending political meetings.

The federal government attempted to control such terrorism with the passage of three Enforcement Acts in 1870 and 1871; the deployment of more troops to the South; and the arrests, fines, and trials of scores of alleged offenders. The efforts did little but publicize the extent of

Southern resistance to reconstruction. Attempts at intimidation successfully continued for decades thereafter. In the meantime, Northerners began to lose interest in remaking the South. By 1877, when Reconstruction formally ended, former Confederates had regained power and control in virtually every Southern state, and blacks had begun to lose many of the civil rights they had enjoyed under Radical Reconstruction.

"Reunited in Brotherly Love"

The North won the war and abolished slavery but lost the battle to create a new South. Decades passed, and blacks struggled to adjust to society that promised them freedom but denied them equality. The Southern economy began to rebuild, but it lagged behind the industrial North despite everyone's best efforts. White Southerners lived with bitter memories of division and defeat that only slowly faded with the passing years.

As time went on, however, the nation inevitably began to reunite. War wounds healed. Old grievances gave way to new tolerance. Dramatic proof of that came in 1913, when the federal government held a fiftieth anniversary reunion of the Battle of Gettysburg, celebrated on the site, to which came thousands of veterans from both North and South.

Southern blacks exercise their right to vote. When Reconstruction ended, blacks had begun to lose many of the civil rights they had won at the end of the Civil War.

One part of the celebration was a reenactment of Pickett's Charge, that tragic dash that had cost so many Southern lives years before. As hundreds of spectators looked on, former members of the Union army took their place on Cemetery Hill, while across the valley, onetime Confederates gathered in the woods and then began their fateful march through the grainfield. Canes and crutches took the place of rifles and bayonets, and many men, bent by age, had to help their comrades up the slope to where the Northern line waited. The tension built as everyone relived the dread and the horror of that long ago conflict.

At a reunion held at the fiftieth anniversary of the Battle of Gettysburg, former enemies shake hands.

As the Confederates neared the top of the hill, they let loose with a rousing rebel yell, not as spine chilling as it had been in 1863, but effective just the same. On hearing the yell, a gigantic gasp rose from the Union men. "It was then," one spectator wrote, "that the Yankees, unable to restrain themselves longer, burst from behind the stone wall, and flung themselves upon their former enemies,"

not to attack, but to embrace and be "reunited in brotherly love and affection." [197]

To these men, as to others like them, the battles of the Civil War had become a thing of the past. Their country was the United States, and for everyone, it was now indeed one nation, indivisible.

★ Notes ★

Introduction: Fort Sumter and Beyond

1. William C. Davis, *Brother Against Brother, The War Begins*. Alexandria, VA: Time-Life, 1983, p. 161.
2. Quoted in Shelby Foote, *The Civil War, A Narrative*, vol. 1. New York: Random House, 1974, p. 39.
3. Quoted in Geoffrey C. Ward, *The Civil War, An Illustrated History*. New York: Knopf, 1990, p. 166.
4. Quoted in Ward, *The Civil War, An Illustrated History*, p. 26.
5. Quoted in William C. Davis, ed., *Great Battles of the Civil War*. New York: Gallery Books, 1984, p. 43.
6. Quoted in Davis, *Great Battles of the Civil War*, p. 43.
7. Quoted in Ward, *The Civil War, An Illustrated History*, p. 39.
8. Quoted in Foote, *The Civil War, A Narrative*, vol. 1, p. 51.
9. Quoted in Ward, *The Civil War, An Illustrated History*, p. 267.
10. Quoted in Ward, *The Civil War, An Illustrated History*, p. 212.

Chapter 1: First Battle of Bull Run

11. Quoted in Ward, *The Civil War, An Illustrated History*, p. 62.
12. Quoted in Foote, *The Civil War, A Narrative*, vol. 1, p. 71.
13. Quoted in Ward, *The Civil War, An Illustrated History*, pp. 62, 64.
14. Quoted in Ward, *The Civil War, An Illustrated History*, p. 64.
15. Quoted in Ward, *The Civil War, An Illustrated History*, p. 64.
16. Quoted in Foote, *The Civil War, A Narrative*, vol. 1, p. 77.
17. Quoted in Ward, *The Civil War, An Illustrated History*, p. 65.
18. Quoted in Ward, *The Civil War, An Illustrated History*, pp. 66–67.
19. Quoted in Davis, *Great Battles of the Civil War*, p. 72.
20. Quoted in Foote, *The Civil War, A Narrative*, vol. 1, p. 80.
21. Quoted in Davis, *Great Battles of the Civil War*, p. 80.
22. Quoted in Davis, *Great Battles of the Civil War*, p. 80.
23. Quoted in Ward, *The Civil War, An Illustrated History*, p. 68.
24. Quoted in Ward, *The Civil War, An Illustrated History*, p. 69.
25. Quoted in Ward, *The Civil War, An Illustrated History*, p. 69.
26. Quoted in Foote, *The Civil War, A Narrative*, vol. 1, p. 83.

27. Quoted in Ward, *The Civil War, An Illustrated History*, p. 69.

28. Quoted in Ward, *The Civil War, An Illustrated History*, p. 67.

29. Bruce Catton, *Reflections on the Civil War*. New York: Doubleday, 1981, p. 231.

30. Quoted in Ward, *The Civil War, An Illustrated History*, p. 69.

31. Quoted in Foote, *The Civil War, A Narrative*, vol. 1, p. 85.

32. Quoted in Ward, *The Civil War, An Illustrated History*, p. 69.

33. Quoted in Foote, *The Civil War, A Narrative*, vol. 1, p. 86.

Chapter 2: Battle of the Ironclads

34. Quoted in A. A. Hoehling, *Thunder at Hampton Roads*. Englewood Cliffs, NJ: Prentice-Hall, 1976, p. 38.

35. Quoted in Hoehling, *Thunder at Hampton Roads*, p. 57.

36. Quoted in Foote, *The Civil War, A Narrative*, vol. 1, p. 255.

37. Quoted in Foote, *The Civil War, A Narrative*, vol. 1, p. 255.

38. Bruce Catton, *Terrible Swift Sword*. New York: Doubleday, 1963, p. 207.

39. Quoted in Ward, *The Civil War, An Illustrated History*, p. 100.

40. Foote, *The Civil War, A Narrative*, vol. 1, p. 257.

41. Quoted in Foote, *The Civil War, A Narrative*, vol. 1, p. 258.

42. Quoted in Hoehling, *Thunder at Hampton Roads*, p. 47.

43. Quoted in Ward, *The Civil War, An Illustrated History*, p. 99.

44. Quoted in Foote, *The Civil War, A Narrative*, vol. 1, p. 259.

45. Quoted in Foote, *The Civil War, A Narrative*, vol. 1, p. 260.

46. Quoted in Hoehling, *Thunder at Hampton Roads*, p. 166.

47. Quoted in Hoehling, *Thunder at Hampton Roads*, p. 192.

48. Quoted in Hoehling, *Thunder at Hampton Roads*, p. 183.

49. Quoted in Hoehling, *Thunder at Hampton Roads*, p. 171.

Chapter 3: Battle of Antietam

50. Quoted in Ward, *The Civil War, An Illustrated History*, p. 139.

51. Quoted in Ward, *The Civil War, An Illustrated History*, p. 284.

52. Quoted in Ward, *The Civil War, An Illustrated History*, p. 284.

53. Quoted in Ward, *The Civil War, An Illustrated History*, p. 147.

54. Quoted in Ward, *The Civil War, An Illustrated History*, p. 151.

55. Quoted in Ward, *The Civil War, An Illustrated History*, p. 152.

56. Quoted in Ward, *The Civil War, An Illustrated History*, p. 272.

57. Quoted in Ward, *The Civil War, An Illustrated History*, p. 154.

58. Quoted in Ward, *The Civil War, An Illustrated History*, p. 158.

59. Albert Marrin, *Virginia's General*. New York: Atheneum, 1994, p. 81.

60. Quoted in Foote, *The Civil War, A Narrative*, vol. 1, p. 702.

61. Quoted in Ward, *The Civil War, An Illustrated History*, p. 158.
62. Quoted in Ward, *The Civil War, An Illustrated History*, p. 158.
63. Quoted in Catton, *Terrible Swift Sword*, p. 457.
64. Quoted in Ward, *The Civil War, An Illustrated History*, p. 160.
65. Foote, *The Civil War, A Narrative*, vol. 1, p. 701.
66. Quoted in Ward, *The Civil War, An Illustrated History*, p. 164.
67. Quoted in Davis, *Great Battles of the Civil War*, p. 221.
68. Quoted in Foote, *The Civil War, A Narrative*, vol. 1, p. 702.
69. Quoted in Ward, *The Civil War, An Illustrated History*, pp. 160, 164.
70. Quoted in Ward, *The Civil War, An Illustrated History*, p. 296.
71. Quoted in Foote, *The Civil War, A Narrative*, vol. 1, p. 707.
72. Quoted in Ward, *The Civil War, An Illustrated History*, p. 249.
73. Quoted in Ward, *The Civil War, An Illustrated History*, p. 246.

Chapter 4: Battle of Gettysburg

74. Bruce Catton, *Gettysburg: The Final Fury*. New York: Doubleday, 1974, p. 7.
75. Quoted in Ward, *The Civil War, An Illustrated History*, p. 214.
76. Quoted in Ward, *The Civil War, An Illustrated History*, p. 214.
77. Quoted in Ward, *The Civil War, An Illustrated History*, p. 142.
78. Quoted in Ward, *The Civil War, An Illustrated History*, p. 215.
79. Quoted in Ward, *The Civil War, An Illustrated History*, p. 216.
80. Quoted in Ward, *The Civil War, An Illustrated History*, pp. 224–25.
81. Quoted in Ward, *The Civil War, An Illustrated History*, p. 220.
82. Quoted in Foote, *The Civil War, A Narrative*, vol. 2, p. 530.
83. Quoted in Ward, *The Civil War, An Illustrated History*, p. 228.
84. Catton, *Gettysburg: The Final Fury*, p. 75.
85. Quoted in Ward, *The Civil War, An Illustrated History*, p. 229.
86. Quoted in Ward, *The Civil War, An Illustrated History*, p. 228.
87. Quoted in Ward, *The Civil War, An Illustrated History*, p. 232.
88. Quoted in Ward, *The Civil War, An Illustrated History*, p. 232.
89. Quoted in Foote, *The Civil War, A Narrative*, vol. 2, p. 568.
90. Quoted in Ward, *The Civil War, An Illustrated History*, p. 236.
91. Quoted in Catton, *Gettysburg: The Final Fury*, p. 101.
92. Quoted in Marrin, *Virginia's General*, p. 66.
93. Catton, *Reflections on the Civil War*, p. 129.
94. Quoted in Ward, *The Civil War, An Illustrated History*, p. 262.

Chapter 5: Siege of Vicksburg

95. Quoted in Davis, *Great Battles of the Civil War*, p. 320.

96. Quoted in Ward, *The Civil War, An Illustrated History*, p. 281.

97. Quoted in Ward, *The Civil War, An Illustrated History*, p. 281.

98. Quoted in Ward, *The Civil War, An Illustrated History*, p. 212.

99. Quoted in A. A. Hoehling, *Vicksburg: 47 Days of Siege*. Englewood Cliffs, NJ: Prentice-Hall, 1969, p. 177.

100. Quoted in Hoehling, *Vicksburg: 47 Days of Siege*, p. 31.

101. Quoted in Ward, *The Civil War, An Illustrated History*, p. 238.

102. Quoted in Hoehling, *Vicksburg: 47 Days of Siege*, p. 134.

103. Quoted in Ward, *The Civil War, An Illustrated History*, p. 238.

104. Quoted in Hoehling, *Vicksburg: 47 Days of Siege*, p. 74.

105. Quoted in Ward, *The Civil War, An Illustrated History*, p. 238.

106. Quoted in Hoehling, *Vicksburg: 47 Days of Siege*, p. 60.

107. Quoted in Ward, *The Civil War, An Illustrated History*, p. 184.

108. Quoted in Hoehling, *Vicksburg: 47 Days of Siege*, pp. 226–27.

109. Quoted in Hoehling, *Vicksburg: 47 Days of Siege*, pp. 241–42.

110. Quoted in Ward, *The Civil War, An Illustrated History*, p. 241.

111. Quoted in Hoehling, *Vicksburg: 47 Days of Siege*, p. 291.

112. Quoted in Davis, *Great Battles of the Civil War*, p. 356.

113. Quoted in Hoehling, *Vicksburg: 47 Days of Siege*, p. 279.

114. Quoted in Hoehling, *Vicksburg: 47 Days of Siege*, p. 281.

115. Quoted in Davis, *Great Battles of the Civil War*, p. 359.

116. Quoted in Ward, *The Civil War, An Illustrated History*, p. 242.

Chapter 6: Battle of Cold Harbor

117. Quoted in T. Harry Williams, *McClellan, Sherman, and Grant*. New Brunswick, NJ: Rutgers University Press, 1962, p. 105.

118. Quoted in Ward, *The Civil War, An Illustrated History*, p. 294.

119. Quoted in Gregory Jaynes, *The Killing Ground, Wilderness to Cold Harbor*. Alexandria, VA: Time-Life, 1986, p. 153.

120. Quoted in R. Wayne Maney, *Marching to Cold Harbor, Victory and Failure*. Shippensburg, PA: White Mane Publishing, 1995, p. 106.

121. Quoted in Maney, *Marching to Cold Harbor, Victory and Failure*, p. 116.

122. Quoted in Jaynes, *The Killing Ground, Wilderness to Cold Harbor*, p. 156.

123. Quoted in Jaynes, *The Killing Ground, Wilderness to Cold Harbor*, p. 156.

124. Quoted in Foote, *The Civil War, A Narrative*, vol. 3, p. 290.

125. Quoted in Foote, *The Civil War, A Narrative*, vol. 3, p. 290.

126. Quoted in Foote, *The Civil War, A Narrative*, vol. 3, p. 289.

127. Quoted in Foote, *The Civil War, A Narrative*, vol. 3, p. 289.

128. Quoted in Noah Andre Trudeau,

Bloody Roads South. Boston: Little, Brown, 1989, p. 282.

129. Jaynes, *The Killing Ground, Wilderness to Cold Harbor,* p. 157.

130. Quoted in Ward, *The Civil War, An Illustrated History,* p. 294.

131. Quoted in Maney, *Marching to Cold Harbor, Victory and Failure,* p. 151.

132. Quoted in Ward, *The Civil War, An Illustrated History,* p. 294.

133. Quoted in Trudeau, *Bloody Roads South,* p. 294.

134. Quoted in Jaynes, *The Killing Ground, Wilderness to Cold Harbor,* p. 161.

135. Quoted in Jaynes, *The Killing Ground, Wilderness to Cold Harbor,* p. 166.

136. Foote, *The Civil War, A Narrative,* vol. 3, p. 292.

137. Quoted in Foote, *The Civil War, A Narrative,* vol. 3, p. 292.

138. Quoted in Jaynes, *The Killing Ground, Wilderness to Cold Harbor,* p. 167.

139. Quoted in Trudeau, *Bloody Roads South,* p. 304.

140. Quoted in Foote, *The Civil War, A Narrative,* vol. 3, p. 295.

141. Quoted in Foote, *The Civil War, A Narrative,* vol. 3, p. 293.

142. Quoted in Foote, *The Civil War, A Narrative,* vol. 3, p. 294.

143. Quoted in Jaynes, *The Killing Ground, Wilderness to Cold Harbor,* p. 167.

144. Quoted in Foote, *The Civil War, A Narrative,* vol. 3, p. 295.

145. Quoted in Ward, *The Civil War, An Illustrated History,* p. 304.

146. Quoted in Jaynes, *The Killing Ground,*

Wilderness to Cold Harbor, p. 169.

147. Quoted in Maney, *Marching to Cold Harbor, Victory and Failure,* p. 192.

148. Quoted in Burke Davis, *Sherman's March.* New York: Random House, 1980, p. 23.

Chapter 7: Sherman's March

149. Quoted in Foote, *The Civil War, A Narrative,* vol. 3, p. 318.

150. Quoted in Williams, *McClellan, Sherman, and Grant,* p. 74.

151. Quoted in Foote, *The Civil War, A Narrative,* vol. 3, p. 319.

152. Foote, *The Civil War, A Narrative,* vol. 3, p. 319.

153. Quoted in Foote, *The Civil War, A Narrative,* vol. 3, p. 320.

154. Quoted in Ward, *The Civil War, An Illustrated History,* p. 322.

155. Quoted in Ward, *The Civil War, An Illustrated History,* p. 324.

156. Quoted in Davis, *Sherman's March,* p. 19.

157. Quoted in Foote, *The Civil War, A Narrative,* vol. 3, p. 411.

158. Quoted in Ward, *The Civil War, An Illustrated History,* p. 326.

159. Quoted in Ward, *The Civil War, An Illustrated History,* p. 325.

160. Quoted in Ward, *The Civil War, An Illustrated History,* pp. 324–25.

161. Quoted in Ward, *The Civil War, An Illustrated History,* p. 327.

162. Quoted in Ward, *The Civil War, An Illustrated History,* pp. 327–29.

163. Quoted in Davis, *Sherman's March,* p. 20.

164. Quoted in Ward, *The Civil War, An Illustrated History*, p. 329.

165. Quoted in Davis, *Sherman's March*, p. 21.

166. Quoted in Foote, *The Civil War, A Narrative*, vol. 3, p. 641.

167. Quoted in Davis, *Sherman's March*, pp. 23, 25.

168. Quoted in Foote, *The Civil War, A Narrative*, vol. 3, p. 641.

169. Quoted in Ward, *The Civil War, An Illustrated History*, p. 343.

170. Quoted in Foote, *The Civil War, A Narrative*, vol. 3, p. 643.

171. Quoted in Marrin, *Virginia's General*, p. 175.

172. Quoted in Williams, *McClellan, Sherman and Grant*, p. 75.

173. Quoted in Ward, *The Civil War, An Illustrated History*, p. 344.

174. Quoted in Foote, *The Civil War, A Narrative*, vol. 3, p. 646.

175. Quoted in Foote, *The Civil War, A Narrative*, vol. 3, pp. 646–47.

176. Quoted in Ward, *The Civil War, An Illustrated History*, p. 348.

177. Quoted in Foote, *The Civil War, A Narrative*, vol. 3, p. 649.

178. Quoted in Foote, *The Civil War, A Narrative*, vol. 3, p. 650.

179. Quoted in Foote, *The Civil War, A Narrative*, vol. 3, p. 650.

180. Quoted in Davis, *Sherman's March*, p. 118.

181. Quoted in Ward, *The Civil War, An Illustrated History*, p. 356.

182. Quoted in Ward, *The Civil War, An Illustrated History*, p. 356.

183. Quoted in Foote, *The Civil War, A Narrative*, vol. 3, p. 794.

184. Quoted in Foote, *The Civil War, A Narrative*, vol. 3, p. 795.

185. Quoted in Foote, *The Civil War, A Narrative*, vol. 3, p. 818.

186. Quoted in Davis, *Sherman's March*, p. 238.

187. Quoted in Foote, *The Civil War, A Narrative*, vol. 3, p. 835.

188. Davis, *Sherman's March*, pp. 241–42.

189. Quoted in Foote, *The Civil War, A Narrative*, vol. 3, p. 989.

190. Quoted in Davis, *Sherman's March*, p. 284.

Chapter 8: Battle for Restoration

191. Quoted in Foote, *The Civil War, A Narrative*, vol. 3, p. 948.

192. Quoted in Foote, *The Civil War, A Narrative*, vol. 3, p. 960.

193. Bruce Catton, *This Hallowed Ground*. New York: Doubleday, 1956, p. 396.

194. Quoted in Richard W. Murphy, *The Nation Reunited, War's Aftermath*. Alexandria, VA: Time-Life, 1987, p. 29.

195. Quoted in Murphy, *The Nation Reunited, War's Aftermath*, p. 61.

196. Quoted in Foote, *The Civil War, A Narrative*, vol. 3, p. 1044.

197. Quoted in Ward, *The Civil War, An Illustrated History*, p. 412.

★ Glossary ★

artillery: Large-caliber weapons, such as cannon; in the U.S. military, an arm of the service designed to operate such weapons.

battery: A fortification equipped with heavy artillery.

breastwork: Temporary, quickly constructed fortification, usually breast-high.

brigade: Formerly a military unit consisting of about four regiments, approximately four thousand men.

canister: Metal cylinder packed with shot that scatter when the cylinder is fired.

casualty: Person injured, killed, captured, or missing in military action.

cavalry: Troops trained to fight on horseback.

company: A small body of troops composed of about one hundred to one hundred fifty men.

corps: Military unit usually made up of two or more divisions; twenty to forty thousand men.

division: An army unit larger than a regiment and smaller than a corps. Approximately twelve thousand men.

enfilade: *n.* gunfire directed along the length of a target. *v.* to sweep with gunfire the whole length of a target.

Federals: Soldiers loyal to the Union cause.

flank: *n.* the right or left end of a formation or force such as an army. *v.* to go around the side of an enemy force.

fortification: A fortified place such as a fort, or any man-made or natural defense such as an earthwork, wall, steep hill, or impassable marsh.

frigate: A high-speed, medium-sized sailing warship of the seventeenth, eighteenth, and nineteenth centuries.

infantry: Combat arm of the army trained to fight on foot.

line: A formation in which the elements are abreast of each other.

matériel: Equipment and supplies of a military force.

mortar: A short-barreled cannon that throws projectiles at high angles.

parapet: The top of a fortification.

platoon: A subdivision of a company.

pontoon bridge: Bridge supported by floating hollow cylinders.

projectile: Object propelled from a firearm, cannon, or other weapon; includes solid shot, shell, and canister.

rampart: A defensive embankment or fortification, often with a parapet on top.

Reconstruction: The period 1865–77, during which the states of the Confederacy were controlled by the federal government before being readmitted to the Union.

regiment: Military unit made up of ten companies and forming a basic element of a division. Approximately one thousand men.

sectionalism: Narrow-minded devotion to the interests and customs of one section of the country.

shell: Hollow projectile containing an explosive charge; a piece of ammunition.

shrapnel: An artillery shell containing metal balls designed to explode in the air above enemy troops.

siege: The surrounding and blockading of a city, town, or fortress by an army attempting to capture it.

skirmish: Minor engagement in a war, usually made by infantry troops.

volley: A discharge of a number of shots or missiles.

★ For Further Reading ★

An extensive amount of information on the Civil War can be accessed on the Internet under American Civil War, or at the following addresses:

www.civilwarhome.com/

www.cwc.lsu.edu/

http://sunsite.utk.edu/civil-war/

Timothy Levi Biel, *The Civil War.* San Diego, CA: Lucent, 1991. An overview of the Civil War from its roots to its conclusion at Appomattox Court House.

Bruce Catton, *Gettysburg: The Final Fury.* New York: Doubleday, 1974. A concise, well-written account of the Battle of Gettysburg, written by a Pulitzer Prize–winning author.

———, *Reflections on the Civil War.* New York: Doubleday, 1981. Fascinating discussion of various war topics ranging from army food to Abraham Lincoln, slavery to submarines.

Albert Marrin, *Unconditional Surrender.* New York: Atheneum, 1994. Biography of Ulysses Grant from his birth to his death due to throat cancer in 1885.

———, *Virginia's General.* New York: Atheneum, 1994. An excellent, concise biography of Robert E. Lee that also contains a wealth of information on the Civil War.

Richard W. Murphy, *The Nation Reunited, War's Aftermath.* Alexandria, VA: Time-Life, 1987. A discussion of life during Reconstruction. Illustrations and photos help illuminate events such as President Andrew Johnson's impeachment, the Ku Klux Klan, and the nation's Centennial celebration in 1876.

James P. Reger, *The Battle of Antietam.* San Diego, CA: Lucent, 1997. Account of one of the bloodiest battles of the Civil War.

☆ Works Consulted ☆

Bruce Catton, *Terrible Swift Sword.* New York: Doubleday, 1963. The second volume of Catton's Centennial History of the Civil War series. Well written and worth reading.

————, *This Hallowed Ground.* New York: Doubleday, 1956. Excellent overview of the Civil War from the North's perspective.

Burke Davis, *Sherman's March.* New York: Random House, 1980. Complete account of Sherman's march through Georgia and the Carolinas.

William C. Davis, *Battle at Bull Run.* New York: Doubleday, 1977. A compelling and complete history of the first major campaign of the Civil War.

————, *Brother Against Brother, The War Begins.* Alexandria, VA: Time-Life, 1983. A reader-friendly volume that details the opening days of the Civil War as well as the issues that led to the conflict. Contains numerous illustrations and photos.

William C. Davis, ed., *Great Battles of the Civil War.* New York: Gallery Books, 1984. Comprehensive account of nineteen major battles of the war, documented with primary source letters, newspaper articles, maps, and quotes.

Clifford Dowdey, ed., *The War Time Papers of R. E. Lee.* Boston: Little, Brown, 1961. Includes Robert E. Lee's official correspondence—letters, orders, dispatches, and battle reports—plus letters to his family. Provides a glimpse into the mind of one of the South's most beloved heroes.

Shelby Foote, *The Civil War, A Narrative.* 3 vols. New York: Random House, 1974. Foote's three-volume work gives a vivid, understandable overview of people, battles, and issues. Well written and includes much fascinating detail.

John Hope Franklin, *Reconstruction, After the Civil War.* Chicago: University of Chicago Press, 1961. An examination of the issues, attitudes, and actions that combined to create the tumultuous twelve-year period known as Reconstruction.

A. A. Hoehling, *Thunder at Hampton Roads.* Englewood Cliffs, NJ: Prentice-Hall, 1976. The author details the creation of the now-famous ironclad warships USS *Monitor* and CSS *Virginia,* then relates the famous clash between the two that changed the face of naval warfare forever.

————, *Vicksburg: 47 Days of Siege.* Englewood Cliffs, NJ: Prentice-Hall, 1969. An account of the siege of Vicksburg through the eyes of some of its participants, including a young bride, a minister's wife and children, a reporter, a soldier's wife, and various others.

Gregory Jaynes, *The Killing Ground, Wilderness to Cold Harbor.* Alexandria, VA: Time-Life, 1986. Brief, well-illustrated overview of U. S. Grant's bloody campaign against R. E. Lee, from the Battle of the Wilderness to the disaster at Cold Harbor.

R. Wayne Maney, *Marching to Cold Harbor, Victory and Failure.* Shippensburg, PA: White Mane Publishing, 1995. An account of the Battle of Cold Harbor in the words of the soldiers and commanders who took part in the disastrous engagement.

Harold Elk Straubing, ed., *In Hospital and Camp: The Civil War Through the Eyes of Its Doctors and Nurses.* Harrisburg, PA: Stackpole Books, 1993. First-person accounts of the trials and triumphs of medical professionals during the war. Includes articles by poet Walt Whitman and author Louisa May Alcott (*Little Women*), both of whom served as hospital volunteers.

Noah Andre Trudeau, *Bloody Roads South.* Boston: Little, Brown, 1989. Dramatic history of Grant's 1864 Virginia campaign from the Wilderness to Cold Harbor.

———, *Like Men of War.* Boston: Little, Brown, 1998. Complete history of black soldiers in the Civil War beginning with the first unofficial ex-slave regiments organized in 1861.

Geoffrey C. Ward, *The Civil War, An Illustrated History.* New York: Knopf, 1990. Fascinating account of the Civil War, complete with extensive period photos. Companion volume to the PBS television documentary series *The Civil War* by Ken and Ric Burns.

T. Harry Williams, *McClellan, Sherman, and Grant.* New Brunswick, NJ: Rutgers University Press, 1962. Brief look at the careers of three Union generals and how their characters affected their generalship during the Civil War.

☆ Index ☆

★ **Picture Credits** ★

✯ About the Author ✯

Like many Americans, Diane Yancey finds the Civil War one of the most fascinating and romantic periods of U.S. history. She is the author of *Civil War Generals of the Union* and *Leaders of the North and South*. Along with her interest in writing and the Civil War, the author likes to collect old books, travel, and enjoy life in the Pacific Northwest with her husband, two daughters, and two cats. Her other books include *Desperadoes and Dynamite*, *The Hunt for Hidden Killers*, *Camels for Uncle Sam*, *Life in a Japanese-American Internment Camp*, and *Life in Charles Dickens's England*.